LETTERS FROM
A YOUNG SHAKER

LETTERS FROM
A YOUNG SHAKER

*William S. Byrd at
Pleasant Hill*

EDITED BY
STEPHEN J. STEIN

THE UNIVERSITY PRESS OF KENTUCKY

Library of Congress Cataloging in Publication Data

Byrd, William S., 1806–1829.
  Letters from a young shaker.

  Bibliography: p.
  Includes index.
  1. Byrd, William S., 1806–1829. 2. Shakers—Kentucky
—Pleasant Hill—Correspondence. 3. Pleasant Hill (Ky.)—
Church history. I. Stein, Stephen J., 1940–
II. Title.
BX9793.B97A4 1985   289′.8′0924 [B]   84-27014
ISBN 0-8131-1542-6

CONTENTS

ILLUSTRATIONS

For three special persons
DEVONIA
BETH ANN
and
STEPHEN MICHAEL

PREFACE

It is my intention to let a voice from the Shaker past speak in this volume, a voice never heard before outside the confines of family and community. I first discovered the remarkable letters of William S. Byrd, the subject of this study, several years ago while preparing the bibliography for a course on marginal religious communities in America. Those who study the history of such sects frequently complain that the membership is silent and that the evaluation of sectarian ideology and activity depends too heavily upon statements from the leadership. Rarely, it seems, does one encounter a cache of primary materials directly from the hands of a follower. Even less frequently are such items written in an articulate, coherent fashion. William S. Byrd's letters are truly an exception to the pattern.

The correspondence of this young man conveys the spirit and mentality of the Shaker society in the early nineteenth century as well as the trials involved with conversion to a socially-unacceptable religion in the young republic. Emotions and convictions were the stuff of religious discourse in that day, but reason too found a place in Byrd's communications. His epistles offer an unusual view into the thought and activity of the western Shakers. Through the pages of Byrd's letters the Shaker experience is humanized, rationalized, and brought to life.

I want to acknowledge the contributions to this project made by a number of persons. I wish to thank the staff of the Lilly Library at Indiana University for their assistance and for permission to publish the texts of the letters and

other items from their collections. Earl D. Wallace provided me with a copy of the deed to the Byrd farm. Several
colleagues have read the introductory essay and have provided helpful criticism. In particular, I wish to mention
David H. Smith and J. Samuel Preus. The members of the
research seminar who gathered at Pleasant Hill in the
spring of 1984 to discuss the development of Shakerism,
especially Brother Theodore E. Johnson, Stephen A. Marini, and Diane Sasson, also contributed to the evolution of
this volume. None of these persons bears responsibility for
the judgments expressed in this work. The students at Indiana University who have encouraged my interest in the
Shakers by their positive response to the story of the society must be mentioned. Three deserve special notice because of their own research in the area: Christy Ramage,
Hilary Selby-Polk, and John Wolford.

Finally, my family—to whom this book is dedicated—
has continued to show patience and understanding, both
of which are necessary for support of the scholarly and human enterprises. My thanks extend especially to them.

INTRODUCTION

In the summer of 1826 the Shaker ministry at Pleasant Hill, Kentucky, reported the arrival of "a nice young Man" who came to their village "and opened his mind." The elders took special notice of the new arrival because "for a long time" there had been "but little ingathering from the world." Occasionally, they noted, "one will drop in, who have mard themselves in the world in some way or other, and once in a while, one will come in who are considered to be in honourable standing in the world; but not more of all, then to keep up our number of believers." For the Shaker communities in the West, the days of rapid expansion were past. By the third decade of the nineteenth century few individuals wished to join the United Society of Believers in Christ's Second Appearing, and even fewer of those who did were persons of "honourable standing."[1]

The young man who received this special attention was William S. Byrd (1806-1829), a descendant of the prestigious Byrd family of Virginia, distinguished for more than four generations by its wealth, prominence, and leadership in American society. William's father, the ministry reported, was a judge of the United States District Court in Ohio. He had left Virginia near the end of the eighteenth century to seek his fortune in the Ohio River Valley. Judge Charles Willing Byrd (1770-1828) became intimately acquainted with the Shakers during the summer of 1825 when a mob, which included some of his relatives, attacked the community at Pleasant Hill. As a result of that assault, he began to investigate the faith and the practice of the Believers. According to the ministry, Judge Byrd became persuaded of the truth of the Shakers' claims and planned eventually to join the society. In the meantime, stirred by his father's investigations, William S. Byrd's interest in the Shakers blossomed and led to his taking up residence among the Believers in Kentucky in mid-June of 1826. Less than a week later he wrote a first letter to his father in Sinking Spring, Ohio, telling of his arrival at Pleasant Hill and of his initial adjustment to community life. Father and son subsequently exchanged correspondence regularly for more than two years, an exchange brought to a halt by the death of the Judge in mid-1828. Nineteen letters written by Byrd to his father from Pleasant Hill are extant in a collection of family papers in the Lilly Library at Indiana University.[2]

William S. Byrd's letters provide a unique vantage point for examining several issues of significance in Shaker history: the religious experiences of an articulate young Shaker in the 1820s, the circumstances of the community at Pleasant Hill during a period of unusual turmoil, and the general situation of the United Society of Believers in the Ohio River Valley two decades after its expansion into the West. The letters reflect, for example, the internal and external stress accompanying Byrd's religious quest. At times he writes with passion about his experiences; at other times he displays almost cold detachment from his own situation. His view of the community at Pleasant Hill seems equally mixed. In some letters he is barely able to contain his zeal and enthusiasm as a new convert; in others he appears to be looking in upon the scene. Byrd struggled to be accepted by the community, and yet he retained strong affection for the members of his natural family. When he first settled at Pleasant Hill he displayed some ambivalence toward the society, but soon he became a skillful advocate for Shaker doctrine. In his letters he constantly defended and interpreted the beliefs and practices of the Believers to his father, whose dedication and commitment, although genuine, were not as total as his own.[3]

Potentially the most puzzling part of William S. Byrd's story involves his reasons for joining the Shakers, a religious sect located on the fringe of American life, a celibate society denounced by critics and attacked by mobs. He gave up a great deal with his decision to join the Believers. Gifted in mind, skilled with words, enjoying considerable advantage by virtue of family position, young Byrd might have prospered in agriculture or commerce, law or government. Instead he elected a way of life at striking variance with that of the men of affairs who were his ancestors. He determined to embody his new faith in consistent practice. He lived the balance of his short life among the Shakers at Pleasant Hill, but he achieved neither prominence nor influence in their ranks. In fact, after two and a half years at the village, Byrd passed from the scene with only the briefest notice, his principal legacy being a series of letters which chronicle his struggle to "bear the cross."[4]

It is tempting, but perhaps risky, to compare the religious experiences of Byrd at Pleasant Hill with those of his more famous contemporaries, such as Joseph Smith, Ralph Waldo Emerson, Orestes Brownson, John Brown, or Theodore Dwight Weld. They too abandoned old patterns of thought for new religious positions, but each of them went on to achieve prominence as prophet, seer, seeker, revolutionary, or reformer. The religious history of the nineteenth century documents their respective contributions. William S. Byrd, by contrast, did not have the opportunity to prove his ultimate worth to the Shaker cause, for he died in 1829, the victim apparently of chronic illness. Nevertheless, it is tantalizing to speculate about the possible role he might have played in the future intellectual leadership of the western Shakers. Byrd clearly possessed a remarkable capacity to write clear and lucid prose. He might well have used his gift to earn a place alongside other prominent Shaker apologists such as John Dunlavy, Benjamin Seth Youngs, and Richard McNemar. All of this, of course, is only speculation and nothing more. From Byrd's letters, however, it is possible to gain a useful picture of the mental and physical world of a talented young Shaker and a passing glimpse into a promising future that was not to be.[5]

FAMILY BACKGROUND

William S. Byrd arrived at Pleasant Hill during a critical moment of transition for the village. By the middle of the 1820s, the early successes of the Believers on the western frontier had ended, and conditions in the Ohio Valley Shaker communities were changing rapidly. For Union Village in Ohio, the center of Shakerism in the West, the peak year numerically was probably 1823. By the middle of the decade all of the Shaker villages in the West were experiencing difficulties, including some decline in membership. The United Society of Believers had grown in the West in part because of a parasitic relationship with the evangelical revivals sweeping through Kentucky, Indiana, and Ohio during the period of the Second Great Awakening. Shaker missionaries from the eastern villages were first attracted to the settlements west of the mountains by reports of the religious excitement in the area. The Believers fed upon the enthusiasm generated by frontier religion. Persons evangelized by mainline revivalists frequently became prospects for subsequent conversion to Shakerism. Consequently the waning of the revivals had the effect of slowing the growth of the communities. Also, as the frontier moved farther west, the lure of abundant cheap land drew settlers from the Ohio Valley. The two Shaker communities in Kentucky—South Union and Pleasant Hill—recorded losses in membership when the Missouri territory was opened to the public in 1825. Additionally, the drain of members by secession or defection was unending. Apostasy constituted a major cause of decline among the communities.[6]

Those who joined the United Society of Believers in the early nineteenth century do not fit easily into any single category. The assumption that the Shakers derived their membership rather exclusively from the ranks of the socially and economically dispossessed is commonplace. According to deprivation theory, the Shakers and other enthusiastic religious groups on the frontier offered refuge and solace to individuals experiencing difficulty in times of social dislocation and cultural transition. One observer notes that "many of the persons converted in the second and third decades of the nineteenth century were, at least partially, motivated by a desire for economic security" and that they "tended to be indifferent to the spiritual aspects" of Shaker life.[7]

Despite some obvious usefulness, deprivation theory contains certain limitations when applied to particular cases. Of late this theoretical construct has been attacked sharply by students of the Shaker experience, who have pointed out that severe economic dispossession was not typical of all converts to Shakerism in the early period. For example, from the use of church rolls and tax records to determine the economic status of the Shaker membership at Harvard, Massachusetts, it has been established that the Believers were "virtually indistinguishable from the rest of the community." There is no evidence to support the assumption that the membership in that village was drawn from a lower social or economic order. In fact, according to the study, the majority of Shakers at Harvard at the end of the eighteenth century were "persons of solid middle income." Proportionately fewer "dependents and poor" existed among the membership than in the town generally. In other words, the Believers came from all classes.[8]

Although equivalent studies of the membership at Pleasant Hill have not yet been carried out, there is reason to believe that the same conclusion will be reached with re-

William Byrd III (1728–1777) and Mary Willing Byrd (1740–1814), grandparents of William S. Byrd. William Byrd III portrait by an unknown artist; Mary Willing Byrd portrait attributed to Matthew Pratt. Both courtesy of Virginia State Library.

spect to it. New studies notwithstanding, the accounts of the leaders at Pleasant Hill cannot be dismissed completely. In 1825 the Shaker ministry reported, "There has been but few gathered in from the world of late, now and then one will come and pretend to want the Gospel, and once in a while a family will come in. Some will stay, and others of them will go away, when they come to feel the cross [i.e., celibacy] a little, so that the number of Believers increases but slowly at present." The elders testified that only occasionally did a person of "honourable standing in the world" join the community. Therefore, even by the standards of the Believers themselves, William S. Byrd was an unusual convert.[9]

The Byrd family of Virginia, to which William belonged even if removed geographically, was the symbol of planter power and influence in America. William Byrd II (1674-1744) was perhaps the most distinguished of Byrd's ancestors. A man of letters and public affairs, his contributions to colonial life were truly significant. He served as a colonial agent for Virginia in England and as a member of the governor's council. He held a variety of other offices, including the post of receiver general, a command in the militia, and a commission as a boundary surveyor. William Byrd II wrote descriptions of his travels and of the natural history of the Virginia area as well as a set of revealing private diaries. In contrast, the extravagances of his son, William Byrd III (1728-1777), including his preoccupation with such genteel amusements as horseracing and cards, resulted in the loss of enormous sums of money and in the consequent reduction of the family estate. Because of his profligacy, substantially fewer resources remained at the disposal of his widow and children after he took his own life in 1777. His family literally saw their fortunes vanish as they presided over the dismantling of the estate and the selling of Westover. His children and grandchildren, in turn, became the first generations in the Byrd family that did not enjoy every advantage of abundant wealth.[10]

These altered circumstances were influential upon the lives of both Charles Byrd and his son William. Charles grew to manhood under the care of relatives in Philadelphia, where he was sent following his father's suicide. He received only a modest inheritance from his parents. The impoverishment of the family was a factor in his decision as a young man to seek his fortune in the western territories. His own assessment of the situation was as follows: "My claim under my father's will—by some, it is supposed to be worth little or nothing—by others, if justice is done, supposed to be of immense value. I suppose myself, that it cannot be worth less than ten thousand dollars, if I should have even the shadow of justice dealt out to me: and that of my mothers, I ought certainly to receive the above mentioned sum of one thousand dollars." Charles's son William S. Byrd never knew at first-hand the affluence of Westover or the enormous power and influence of the Byrd family. His childhood and youth were spent in the less refined circumstances of the emerging frontier society of Ohio and Kentucky.[11]

Nevertheless, William S. Byrd was not a victim of economic deprivation. His father enjoyed relative affluence and exercised considerable political influence throughout the Ohio Valley. When Charles went west, he first established himself as a lawyer in Frankfort, Kentucky. Then in 1797 he married Sarah Meade (1775-1815), a daughter of David Meade of Jessamine County, Kentucky, a former neighbor of the Byrds at Westover. Meade's elegant estate, Chaumiere des Prairies, near Lexington, was the frequent gathering place for former Virginians of Republican persuasion. Sarah's sister, Susan Everard Meade, married Nathaniel Massie, a political ally of Charles Byrd. Eventually Byrd secured an appointment as secretary of the Northwest Territory. Additionally, he served as acting governor of the territory and as a member of the state constitutional convention in 1803 when Ohio was admitted to the union. Subsequently he was appointed by Thomas Jefferson to the federal bench, a post he had coveted for some time. He held the judgeship until his death.[12]

William Byrd's mother, Sarah, seems to have struggled to maintain a Virginian way of life in the more demanding circumstances of the frontier West. She followed planter patterns as far as possible, spending considerable time away from home with her children visiting friends and relatives. She enjoyed the finer things of life, such as the piano Charles brought for her to their home in Cincinnati. She probably devoted much of her time to her children, even though a servant, Lavinia, may have had a primary role in their care. Sarah most likely had some part in the early education of the children, perhaps reading to them children's books. Among the papers is one entitled *Trifles for Children*, a small publication filled with aphorisms. Yet Sarah knew hardship and suffering also. She and Charles lost an infant daughter in 1805 or 1806. Her own early death in 1815, the result of illness, was very painful according to a description rendered by Charles, who watched his wife's condition deteriorate day by day. Despite large doses of medicine, Sarah did not improve. Although she was not a particularly religious person, near the end of her life, wracked by fever and knowing full well that she was about to die, Byrd reported that she began to hear "the most delightful church musick over her head." The Judge took some comfort in retelling this story to his family and friends.[13]

William was one of five children from the marriage who survived infancy. He had two brothers, Kidder Meade and Powel, and two sisters, Mary Willing (known in the family as Molly) and Evelyn Harrison. All carried the names of powerful relatives and political allies. William's middle name, Silouee, was given in honor of an Indian who saved the life of William Byrd III in 1760. Undoubtedly Sarah's death was a most traumatic event for young William. Three years after her death, Charles Byrd remarried. His second wife, the widow Hannah Miles, had several children by her previous marriage. William's relationship with his step-mother was friendly but proper. Charles and Hannah became the parents of two additional children, Samuel Otway and Jane.[14]

William enjoyed the special attention and largess of his grandmother Mary Willing Byrd, who displayed considerable affection for all of Charles's children. Before her death in 1814 she frequently wrote to her grandchildren, offering advice and counsel. In a letter of 1811 she made provision for a gift of $500.00 "for the use of my sweet William Silouee." The money was placed in trust with John Richard, a relative. She intended that her grandson be given the annual interest from the sum to purchase clothing, schooling, and "a few useful books." "When he becomes of age," she wrote, "he may draw the principal, as well as the interest that may then be due." This concern for William's education became a preoccupation of his grandmother.[15]

Nonetheless, the precise nature of William's formal education remains uncertain. Had he been in Virginia, most likely he would have attended the College of William and Mary or the new University of Virginia. Instead, he and his brothers were probably educated in local schools and by tutors until they were old enough to read law with their father or their uncle, Samuel Woodson. Kidder Byrd entered the legal profession in 1824 and tried unsuccessfully to establish a practice, first in Alabama and then in Washington. Powel's unwillingness to consider law as a profession was a source of unending frustration to his father. There is evidence that William had studied enough law to understand the technical procedures involved with dividends and the transfer of property. Whatever his ultimate professional intentions, William was at home in the world of books and letters.[16]

In addition to these family advantages, William enjoyed some financial independence as a result of the settlement of the family estate in Virginia. He held, for example, shares of stock in the Dismal Swamp Land Company, a collective speculative endeavor stemming in part from the activities of his great-grandfather, who was the surveyor of the Virginia-Carolina border. All of the Byrd grandsons had been given shares in the venture. He also owned a number of shares of bank stock. The amount of capital at his disposal was modest in comparison to that controlled by earlier generations of the family, but Byrd was accustomed to think of himself as a man of resources and to conduct his affairs in a manner appropriate to family tradition.[17]

RELIGIOUS BACKGROUND

By contrast with their reputation for social, political, and financial achievements, the members of the Byrd family were rarely celebrated for their religious accomplishments. William Byrd II was typical of many in the family. He reflected a "gentleman's regard for moderation" in religion, his Anglicanism tempered by a rational outlook. For the zeal of the Puritans he had little patience. William Byrd III was not an especially religious man, though he was honest enough to acknowledge that his own "folly & inattention to accounts" had brought on his economic distress. The Byrd women were more inclined to be openly devout and pious. In that respect Charles Byrd favored the female side of the family, for he was very much interested in religion and for years engaged in a search for spiritual peace.[18]

Charles Byrd's religious development was complex. As a small child he first became acquainted with Anglicanism through his family. Following his father's suicide he was placed under the care of Thomas Powell, his mother's brother-in-law, a wealthy Quaker in Philadelphia, where he was exposed to a different set of values. When he went west as a young man, Byrd associated with the Presbyterian Church. In 1815, the year of his wife's death, he experienced a personal conversion to evangelical views. Commenting on the change, he wrote, "I lived 44 years in the world, without knowing the most essential point in religion: it is this, that we are to depend & rest our hopes of salvation, not on our own supposed merit, but on the righteousness of Jesus Christ our blessed Saviour: & tho' holiness on our part is the necessary consequent effect of a Christian life, yet this of itself forms no part of our claim to life everlasting." Increasingly Byrd's life became preoccupied with religious matters and in particular with the Bible. He believed that his new evangelical perspective was compatible with the rationalistic religious principles and moral values he had learned from childhood. Thereafter he combined his religious and philosophical interests informed by the Enlightenment with a deep commitment to evangelical Christianity.[19]

Byrd's religious views influenced his attitudes toward child-rearing, as is evident from a document written for his own use in 1821 entitled "Abridgment of My Advice to My Children on Some Important Subjects." The Judge encouraged his children to pursue a healthy, temperate life-style. He was especially harsh in condemning the use of "strong drinks," which he regarded as "destructive to health" and "replete with every sort of ruin." On the specific question of religion, his advice was the following: "The certain road to vital profitable religion is daily to pray in the name of our Saviour for Gods Holy Spirit, who is graciously promised to all who will ask for him. Luke XI. 13. If this promise is true, then the Bible is true. Can you neglect to make the experiment in a case that involves your present, and what is far more important, your everlasting peace?"[20]

Charles Byrd's enlightened evangelicalism served him well until the fall of 1824. In October of that year he received news that his son Kidder, who was given to "melancholy," had drowned himself in the Potomac River. A few weeks earlier Charles had suggested to his son a way of overcoming depression. "You must keep up your spirits like a man," he wrote, "reflecting that besides it being impoli-

tick to give way to sorrow, especially of that sort, it is both
unmanly and cowardly." Start with prayer, he counseled,
and pray for wisdom. If that fails, indulge in "castlebuild-
ing," that is, "suppose for the time that you should become
healthy and wealthy—then ask yourself, how in that event
would you dispose of your time &c." According to his own
testimony, the "afflictive calamity" of the drowning threw
the Judge into a state of deep depression and disorienta-
tion. His diary entries for the next two years reveal how
central a fixation Kidder's death remained as Charles re-
constructed again and again the circumstances surrounding the event. Kidder's death also dealt a special blow to
William, for he had been very close to his older brother.
They had been correspondents after Kidder's departure
from Sinking Spring.[21]

During the summer following Kidder's death the Judge
became deeply interested in the United Society of Believers. While visiting in-laws in Jessamine County, Kentucky,
he learned of the mob attack upon Pleasant Hill. His subsequent investigations of the society led him to purchase
and read a copy of Benjamin Seth Youngs' *Testimony of
Christ's Second Appearing*, a volume which has been called
"the first authoritative work on the Millennial Church."
Byrd read Youngs' volume several times and then visited
the Shaker community of Union Village, Ohio, in October,
having prepared a list of theological and practical questions to discuss with the Shakers. The ministry gave him
detailed answers and suggested that he read John Dunlavy's *Manifesto*, subsequently regarded by many as "the
definitive treatise on Shaker theology."[22]

These contacts with the Believers persuaded the Judge
of the value of their beliefs and practices. According to his
diary, he visited Union Village again in April 1826, this
time taking William with him. This visit may have been
William's first direct contact with the society. By early May,
Charles Byrd was convinced of the truthfulness of the belief "that Christ had appeard a second time in compliance

with his gracious promise." He also found sufficient "testimony" to confirm other Shaker doctrines. In fact, he felt that the lives of the Believers themselves were the best evidence of the truthfulness of their claims. Within a few months the Judge was firmly committed to the Shaker cause. By the beginning of August he professed that the United Society of Believers was "the only true church of christ."[23]

William's growing interest in the Shakers paralleled that of his father. Unfortunately, frustratingly little information remains concerning the early development of his religious ideas. During childhood the younger Byrd most likely absorbed the enlightened evangelicalism espoused by his father. By 1826 he certainly knew the language of Protestant theology and was familiar with the religious issues that had stirred many people in the West during the early decades of the century, such as the nature of human freedom and responsibility, the character of sin and holiness, and the power of the spirit of God. William was intimately acquainted with several prominent ministers in southern Ohio, including William Williamson and Dyer Burgess, both of whom remained on friendly terms with him throughout his lifetime. By the spring of 1826 William was reading the Shaker volumes recommended to the Judge. In fact, in early May, when William was planning one of his frequent visits to his relatives in Kentucky, he proposed to carry with him a copy of the *Testimony*, which Charles described in a letter as "a literary production of considerable merit." Not long after this visit to Jessamine County, William departed for Pleasant Hill.[24]

One useful commentary on the close relationship between father and son comes from the hand of William Williamson, formerly the family's minister in West Union, Ohio. The same source sheds some light on William's religious instruction as a youth. In 1826 Williamson accused the Judge of having influenced his son to join the Shakers, a charge denied in a friendly but spirited and lengthy letter. Charles Byrd wrote, "My . . . object is to assure you that I have never exercised any parental influence over William, to lead him into the adoption of the construction put upon the Bible by the United Society called Shakers. Prior to his acquaintance with any of the members, and before he had read any one of their books or pamphlets, I prevailed on him to give to the old and New Testament an attentive perusal. He had no other foundation for his theological tenets than what you had given him, and in part the teaching that he received from myself which was still the same thing, as my first religious ideas were imparted to me by you. I gave him the very counsel with which you favored me in your last to pray to God his Holy Spirit, asking in the name of his Son, to enable him profitably to understand the Scriptures." Charles's protest notwithstanding, it appeared to outside observers in 1826 that William had been predisposed and possibly encouraged by his father to travel to Pleasant Hill.[25]

This is the point in the narrative at which the introduction began. By mid-June 1826, William S. Byrd had taken up residence at Pleasant Hill. His father, by contrast, found himself in circumstances which prevented his following the same course of action. As the Judge weighed the obstacles against moving to Pleasant Hill, he had concerns about support for his family, his own poor health, and a possible divorce by Hannah. Charles Byrd regarded himself as a Believer in principle, but he was unable (and possibly unwilling) in 1826 to carry his Shaker principles into practice, even though the prospect of a move to Kentucky was attractive to him because he would be "with William and a society who afford *some evidence* of their being a true branch of Christs church." The dialogue which took place through the months of their correspondence reflects the efforts of the two Byrds to justify and rationalize to each other their respective positions and patterns of action.[26]

EARLY MONTHS AT THE VILLAGE

When William S. Byrd took up residence at Pleasant Hill in 1826, the village already possessed a number of the landmarks still in evidence today at the historical restoration. Located about seven miles from the town of Harrodsburg on the main road to Lexington, Shakertown (as it was also known) sat on a hilltop which gave a commanding view of the surrounding area. The road, traversing directly from east to west, split the village, bringing the residents into daily contact with those who traveled upon it. South of the road the principal structure was the meetinghouse, commonly described by visitors as possessing architectural soundness and unusual properties, including its large open floor, which set it off from more conventional religious buildings. In the meetinghouse the Believers gathered to sing the praises of Christ and Mother Ann and to perform their distinctive dances. North of the road were three large Shaker dwellings constructed of brick and stone. Each of these family houses followed the same basic plan. Directly opposite the meetinghouse, under construction, was a massive stone dwelling which eventually overshadowed the existing buildings in both size and capacity. These buildings, and more to come in the years ahead, were the work of Micajah Burnett, a very talented architect and engineer who was a member of the society. His work added to the reputation of the community.[27]

Scattered throughout the village, which measured approximately 900 feet in length at the road, were numerous other less imposing structures used for shops, offices, barns, and storage buildings. Wide flagstone walks connected the principal edifices with one another. Other houses and buildings were scattered at a distance on the more than 3,000 acres of land owned at the time by the Shakers. Some of these structures had been the original dwellings of the first converts before the village itself was constructed. On the road to the west toward Harrodsburg was located a three-story gristmill at which the Believers processed various agricultural products, including corn and flax. At the opposite end of the village was situated a tavern where travelers and strangers were supplied room and board.

The population of Pleasant Hill in 1826 was less than five hundred residents, divided somewhat equally between the Center, East, and West families. The leadership of the community resided in the ministry, composed of Mother Lucy Smith, who was the dominant religious influence in the village, Elder Samuel Turner, and Elder John R. Bryant (called Brother Rufus), all three long-time Shakers. Mother Lucy had become first in the ministry at Pleasant Hill in 1818. Each of the family units also had its own elders and eldresses, deacons and deaconesses. Soon after his arrival William S. Byrd was placed in the East Family under the leadership of Elder Brother Edmond Bryant and Elder Sister Charity Burnett in a probationary condition reserved for those who had not yet decided to commit themselves fully to the society. The leadership of the community also included trustees who were responsible for the financial affairs of the village and business negotiations with the outside world. The various agricultural and commercial enterprises of the Shakers, relying upon the labor of both male and female members of the community, produced surpluses and commodities which were sold to the non-Shaker population.[28]

Some of the details of this description come from the report of an observer who visited Pleasant Hill in the spring of 1825, approximately one year before William S. Byrd's arrival. That commentator, in rather typical fashion for the day, denounced certain elements of the community's life as repulsive, while commending others. In the last paragraph of his published observations, he summarized his mixed impressions: "I have dwelt the longer on the subject of this community of people, believing that you would be gratified with a minute account of a people so

The East Family Dwelling at Pleasant Hill, built in 1817. William S. Byrd probably lived here during part of his stay at Pleasant Hill.

peculiar in their tenets, so singular in their modes of life, and who blend so much theological absurdity with practical sobriety and common sense, and of whose moral character, I believe so many unjust slanders have been propagated." This was the setting and these were the people that Byrd joined in mid-1826.[29]

Byrd's initial letter to his father sounded a theme which echoes through the whole of the correspondence, his desire to purchase property adjacent to the Shaker village. By mid-June William had reached a level of substantial commitment to the society. His father's response to the request contained both apprehension and skepticism, in answer to which William marshaled a series of arguments over a period of several months. In a fashion typical of the Byrd lineage, he itemized his resources, including bank stocks and shares in the Dismal Swamp venture. He left nothing to chance, spelling out in exact detail the necessary steps to be taken for the sale of the stocks, if his father should agree to dispose of any in accord with the plan. William's proposal called for the purchase of a farm which lay one mile south of the village. In this effort he was counseled and supported by the village trustee, Francis Voris. When William first proposed the purchase, he was very diplomatic and solicitous of his father's authority. One month later he made a passing nod to the same considerations and went on to add a not-so-veiled threat to proceed, no matter what his father decided. "If after the perusal of our letters," William wrote, "you think you can comply with the request made in my last without any inconvenience to yourself, and without any injury to the rest of your family, I will be much pleased. I should be very sorry to go contrary to your advice in any thing, although I have arrived to that time of life when by the laws of our Country the empire of the Father, or other Guardian, gives place to the empire of reason." William's financial dealings were to remain a bone of contention with his father.[30]

Another preoccupation of William in his early letters to

The Meetinghouse at Pleasant Hill, built in 1820, where the Shaker community worshipped. Photo by Katie W. Bullard.

his father was the question of health—his own and his father's—and how best to nurture it. For years William had been a victim of chronic illness. The precise nature of his ailments remains unclear, but his childhood record documents recurrent digestive problems. His father once noted, "Williams having a weak stomach as well as myself, inclines me in some degree to doubt whether it was callamet that debilitated mine." In his initial letter from Pleasant Hill William wrote, "I have suffered with costifness more than usual for some days past, but am somewhat better now." Costifness, a term used commonly in the nineteenth century to describe constipation, was symptomatic of a number of medical problems. Charles frequently recommended treatments of one kind or another. On one occasion he wrote, "William, when I have a convenient opportunity, I think I will persuade him to take senna—if this should not relieve him altogether, I will give him Dandelion tea, with an occasional repetition of the senna—I will if necessary give him the tincture of rhubarb, and often recommend to him the Cummomile flours, either to chew, or in tea." The pursuit of health in the nineteenth century often involved experimentation with various remedies—medicinal, dietary, environmental, and behavioral. All of these approaches are reflected in William's activities and letters. Charles Byrd, who experimented freely with chemical and herbal medicines, offered William advice concerning the relative value of powders, the "blue pill," oil of flaxseed, and rhubarb. William complied rather willingly with his father's counsel, experimenting liberally with various remedies. He also became increasingly concerned about the impact of diet upon physical well-being and began to defend Shaker eating patterns as conducive to health.[31]

William's decision to reside at Pleasant Hill was determined in part by his favorable assessment of the climate and water supply at Shakertown. He and his father carried on an extended discussion of the relative advantages for health of stoves or fireplaces. He filled his letters with descriptions of his physical activity because he subscribed to the view that exercise was necessary for well-being, a theory his father had preached to his children for years. The rule of the Shakers prescribing some kind of manual labor for all members was consistent with William's own ideas on the importance of exercise. Even when he was unable to take part in the heavier tasks traditionally carried out by the male members of the community, he resorted to walking or horseback riding. During his first months at Pleasant Hill he also spent time in the less strenuous activity of reading. This appears to have been confined largely to religious publications, including the Bible, especially the New Testament, and the writings of the Shakers. William, for example, read very closely John Dunlavy's *Manifesto*.[32]

One of the most striking functions of William's early letters to his father is the use he made of them to maintain physical and psychological involvement with his natural family, nuclear and extended, even as he began to identify closely with the Shaker community as his new family. Five of the first six extant letters open with the loving address, "Dear Papa." The closings of the early letters are equally explicit in the statement of overt affection. These forms of familial and filial endearment tempered with the passage of time. Nevertheless, William remained highly solicitous of his father's well-being and concerned with the affairs of the rest of his family. He was always eager to see his father, who visited the village at regular intervals. From time to time William wrote and visited his relatives in nearby Jessamine County, and he corresponded with his siblings.[33]

Despite continuing affection for his natural family, the early letters also reveal William's increasing involvement in the affairs of the community, his Shaker family. By the second letter he has begun to employ the common designation of "brother" for the males of the community. Those in positions of authority and responsibility he identified correctly with titles of honor and respect, such as Mother Lucy and Elder Samuel. Soon he began to write about the members of the Shaker community with expressions of affection rivaling those he employed for his father and natural family. The members of the community, in turn, took care of his physical needs in ways that his father had previously. In particular, Francis Voris, a trustee of the village, assisted with a number of daily needs, including the purchase of furniture and clothing.[34]

The first months at Pleasant Hill marked a crucial period of adjustment for William. Several factors assisted his smooth transition to life at the village. He was assured of his father's approval for the move. Francis Voris took special pains to assist him with practical matters. He also received strong support from other members of the Shaker community. And he lived in the hope of becoming a full member of the society. The challenge and excitement of his new life proved a strong stimulus to him. Nevertheless, these same months taxed William sorely. He was plagued by poor health as he struggled to meet the standards and expectations of his new faith. In November of the first year he wrote, "The work in which I am engaged, that is to put to death my own self, is as I mentioned in my last letter a great work, but difficult as it is, I suppose it would be more so were I in the enjoyment of good mental and bodily health."[35]

ACCEPTANCE INTO THE SOCIETY

By the end of 1826 William Byrd's situation in the community had begun to change in several important ways. In October he and his father purchased jointly the 248-acre farm of William and Priscilla McMurtry, an action in compliance with his persistent request for his father's permission and financial support. William allowed the Shakers to cultivate the land, which bordered their property, without cost. The purchase, unfortunately, did not resolve the conflict with his father, and hard feelings persisted. William became defensive about the transaction and tried to reassure his father that the investment was sound and secure. The situation was made even more complex, however, by William's stated desire to transfer his share of the farm to the community, consistent with his understanding of the implications of his new faith, which called for the sacrifice of all "for christs sake and the gospels." To forsake all literally was the demand placed upon Believers. After he had given up all, William believed, his subsequent needs would be met by the community.[36]

A few months after his arrival in the village, William expressed the desire to be accepted into the "Church," the inner circle of the United Society of Believers. He made his wish known to the ministry at Pleasant Hill through Elder Samuel Turner. The decision of the ministry in his case is very instructive. Repeatedly the Shakers had faced the charge that they had taken advantage of unsuspecting persons and had duped them into joining the society in order to profit from their assets. In the case of Byrd, who was perceived to be a very unusual and attractive convert, the Shaker ministry seemed extra cautious—perhaps, in part, because William's father was a public official and a person of considerable political influence. After deliberation, the ministry at Pleasant Hill decided that it was not "proper" at the moment for William to "sign the covenant" lest the impression be created that he had been taken in "unawares," without sufficient time to judge everything for himself. Disappointed though he was, William consoled himself with the Shakers' assurances "that they would all view me as nearly related to them, and as much one of the body, as if I had actually signed the compact." Thus the leaders of the community managed to avoid publicly the charge of deceit or fraud at the same time that they privately assured William of their close relationship with him.[37]

This setback did not dull William's ardor for the community. On the contrary, these months witnessed his "increasing confidence in Shakerism," a faith nurtured by the full and warm acceptance of the members of the community and by the strong bonds which developed with the leadership. The ministry at Pleasant Hill paid close attention to his activities, as they did theoretically for all members in the community. They were especially interested in the content of the letters which he wrote and received. (They did, however, allow the Byrds limited privacy in their communications.) The ministry recorded their pleasure with William's correspondence and encouraged him to continue writing letters.[38]

During these months of deepening involvement with the Shaker community, William continued to use his letters to maintain communication with the members of his natural family. He corresponded with Charles Byrd in Ohio and with his siblings and relatives elsewhere. Not all of these exchanges were cordial. He found most distasteful, for example, the correspondence with his sister Molly, who had fallen in with bad company. He feared that she might visit Pleasant Hill, causing him grief and embarrassment. William also tried to play the role of mediator between his other sister, Evelyn, and his father. Sometimes Charles Byrd was a hard man to get along with; he could be stern and even violent with his own children. Charles was accustomed to use physical force to discipline his children. For example, on one occasion in 1823 he gave his daughter Jane a "pretty severe slapping to make her cease from crying." On another occasion he came to blows with Powel, who had called him "purvaricating," "a mean old fellow," and a "hypocrite." When Molly, Evelyn, and Powel responded negatively to his decision to accept the Shaker faith, the Judge made his dissatisfaction with them very apparent. William tried to mediate these relationships through his letters. Despite certain discomfort, he also corresponded with members of the Woodson family, relatives on his mother's side in Jessamine County, who were opposed to the Shakers in principle and in practice.[39]

William's letters during these same months reveal his growing acceptance by the members of the community at Pleasant Hill. He frequently conveyed greetings and messages from particular Shakers to Charles and to other members of his natural family. One of the most interesting figures to emerge from the letters is Leonard Jones, a Believer who seems to have played the role of special friend to William and who also exchanged letters with Charles. Jones had joined the community in 1823 after being involved in a public confrontation with a disorderly spectator in the meetinghouse. He quickly acquired a reputation for being "conscientous" and full of zeal. He liked to speak and pray in public, and he was frequently the recipient of visions which he described in detail for others. The ministry at Pleasant Hill concluded that Jones "bids fare to make a useful Man in the Gospel, if he abides faithful." However, from time to time he had problems with faithfulness to the covenant and with his capacity to "bear the cross." Brother Leonard displayed considerable open affection for the Byrds. He often sent greetings to Charles through William. In April 1827, for example, Jones wrote: "I rejoice to find William with an additional strength of Body and Mind, with sound and experimental views, of the separating, cuting off and dying Work, between the flesh, and the spirit. . . . his peace seems to be solid, and the fear of death seems to be removed with him so that I feel he cannot do as well as to abide in obedience where he is." A number of the leaders of the community, including Mother Lucy and others in the ministry, also sent messages to Charles. These relationships were signs of William's fuller integration into the society.[40]

One additional mark of William's growing acceptance was the way in which his letters were increasingly filled with details concerning the situation in the other western Shaker communities. He took note of the arrival and departure of leaders from other villages, such as Benjamin S. Youngs and Richard McNemar. He reflected on the internal condition of the society and on questions of leadership, controversy, and apostasy. In the case of West Union, the Shaker colony at Busro, Indiana, William speculated on the reasons for its failure, which included conflict with Indians, disease, and ineffective leaders. He also kept his father informed on diverse items of local news. By the middle of 1827 William was a young man with two families—one of blood and one of faith. With the passing of time his adopted family began to assume greater importance in his life.[41]

TROUBLE AT PLEASANT HILL

The years of William S. Byrd's residence at Pleasant Hill were not good times for the village. In fact, as his bond with the society grew stronger, the community itself went through a period of turmoil and stress. Already in 1825 a number of members of the community, under the leadership of John Whitbey, were challenging the authority of the ministry, calling for reform of the administrative practices of the village. They wanted more involvement of the Believers in the governance of the community and in the handling of its goods. Whitbey had fallen under the influence of Robert Owen, the Scottish utopian thinker and the founder of New Harmony in nearby Indiana. Whitbey's influence was especially strong among the younger members of the Shaker community. After he was forced to leave Pleasant Hill in November 1825, he traveled to New Harmony. In 1826, with the help of Owenites, he published an attack on the Shakers entitled *Beauties of Priestcraft; or, A Short Account of Shakerism.* In 1827 Whitbey returned to Kentucky to join forces with other Shaker apostates.[42]

Early in the same year a number of organizational changes were made at Pleasant Hill which had the effect of democratizing aspects of life in the village. In particular, the responsibilities of the trustees were redistributed so that each family handled its own resources. But when a

A letter from William S. Byrd to his father, from Pleasant
Hill, December 29, 1826. From the Byrd Papers, Lilly Library,
Indiana University, Bloomington.

delegation was sent to the headquarters of the United Society of Believers in New Lebanon, New York, to secure approval for these changes, that approval was not forthcoming. Pleasant Hill was declared no longer in union with the patterns of the larger society. As a result, a number of Shaker leaders from other communities were sent to visit the village during the summer of 1827. William recorded the arrival and departure of these visiting elders. Soon conflict broke into the open at Shakertown, and a major defection occurred.[43]

The turmoil at Pleasant Hill was apparent in William's letters to his father. Late in May 1827 he wrote of "changes" taking place in the community and of the fact that a number of members had apostatized. Many of the younger order, in particular, had left the society and had married. The effect of this turmoil on William, however, was not destructive. "All this has not discouraged me," he assured his father, "but on the contrary it has rather had a tendency to increase my faith, as it goes to shew that the harvest of the Lord has come, and that his reapers have gone forth." When the situation at Pleasant Hill went from bad to worse in the following months, William sent an urgent letter to his father, asking him to postpone an impending visit to the village because of "great confusion" in the community. Now even William seemed upset with the situation. One week later, after consultation with the ministry, he penned a longer, less disturbed letter, filling in additional details about the confusion at the village.[44]

In the second letter William described the apostasy of many from the society and the resultant discontent and disorder. The elders feared this news might cause Charles Byrd to reevaluate his commitment to the Believers. William therefore attempted to reassure his father that his own position had not been shaken and that rather than being depressed by such events he was able to view them positively, seeing the conflict as cause for joy that "the work of God [is] going on, a work which will make a final

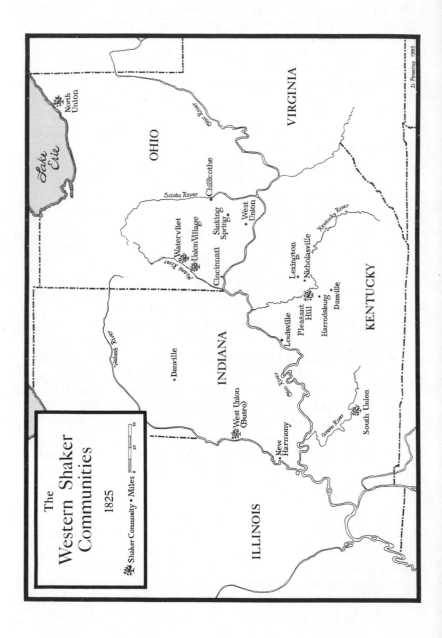

The
Western Shaker
Communities
1825

⚜ Shaker Community • Miles 0 — 25 — 50

D. Pomeroy 1985

Lake Erie

⚜ North Union

OHIO

Ohio River

VIRGINIA

Scioto River • Chillicothe

⚜ Watervliet
⚜ Union Village • Sinking Spring
• West Union
• Cincinnati

Miami River

Lexington •
Nicholasville •

Kentucky River

⚜ Pleasant Hill
• Louisville
• Harrodsburg • Danville

KENTUCKY

Wabash River

• Danville

INDIANA

Ohio River

⚜ West Union (Busro)

• New Harmony

Green River

• South Union

ILLINOIS

separation between good and evil." William affirmed that the period of stress was proof "that there is on Pleasant Hill a righteous, godly people, with whom the wicked cannot dwell." In the same letter William reported some particulars concerning a reorganization in the leadership of the community. Subsequent letters documented further changes as the visiting Shaker leaders sought to bring the village back into conformity with the rest of the society.[45]

Despite these statements of public confidence, William expressed private astonishment at another development. In a letter of March 1828, he reported to his father that Mother Lucy Smith, whose presence and influence had been so dominant at the village for years, had gone to Union Village and was not expected to return to Pleasant Hill. For both Charles and William, Mother Lucy was the paragon of holiness and virtue, a living symbol of the Shaker way of life. She had gained prominence and leadership in the society through her "powerfull testimony" against sin and wickedness and through the example of "the purity of her life and conversation." William initially reported that opposition to her leadership had arisen in connection with the "spirit of evil" manifest in the community. Even in the face of this blow, William was confident that God would prevail over the adversary, purging the church "of all evil, and every thing that is contrary to the nature of God and a life of holiness." Later William was directed by the ministry to add a postscript to his letter, stating that the reason for Mother Lucy's not returning to the village was her "age and infirmity," thereby minimizing the theme of dissension in the ranks of the society.[46]

The Shaker leaders tried to reassure Charles Byrd through William's letters that the situation at Pleasant Hill was under control. At the same time, however, in June William noted that the decline in the membership of the community was continuing. Another immediate impact of the turmoil was an increasing problem with recruiting new members. "There has been but little ingathering of Souls from the world for a long time," the ministry observed, "and the most that do come, are runaways from other societys, and they do not stay long. So we do not look nor wish for many to gather in, in the present state of the society, for if they should, it is most likely they would not stay long." One positive result of the departures, according to William, was some increase of "righteousness and peace" in the village.[47]

Usually William spared his father additional details concerning the apostates, but in the June letter he departed from that practice. He informed Charles Byrd of the surprising fact that Elder James Gass and his wife Lucy— prominent Shaker leaders at Pleasant Hill and personal friends of both Byrds—had suddenly left the community. Indeed, this was a surprising development. For many years James Gass had served as the Elder Brother of the First Order. His wife Lucy was also a leading member of the order. Lucy had been singled out by William for special mention in several letters to the Judge. On one occasion a gift of peaches had been presented to her. Even this astonishing defection, William assured his father, had not affected his faith adversely. Following their departure from the village, Gass joined with another apostate in a legal effort to recover their shares of property from the community, a move which resulted in a prolonged legal battle that was not settled until 1834, when the Circuit Court of Appeals in Kentucky ruled against the claimants and in support of covenanted common property.[48]

A most telling measure of the accuracy of William's description of the turmoil at Pleasant Hill is a contemporary report filed by Elder Benjamin S. Youngs of South Union, one of the Shaker leaders who visited the village during the months of disorder. In September 1828 he wrote a long confidential letter to the ministry at New Lebanon, describing the situation at Pleasant Hill and assessing responsibility for the troubles. Youngs assured the leadership in New York that the "condition" of Pleasant Hill was "not to be despaired of," although it was "deplorable" when compared to that of five or six years earlier. The seeds of "misery and misfortune" had already been present at the earlier time of prosperity, for the Believers at Pleasant Hill had regarded themselves as "superior in gifts and talents" to all other communities in the West. Lucy Smith, he reported, was "applauded their Mother, as a being superior to all others on Earth."[49]

Subsequently, he wrote, a clash of opinions developed as "faultfinders and ismhunters" troubled the community. John Whitbey, whom Youngs called "at heart a perfect infidel," spread contamination in the community. The ministry was attacked, and the leaders lost authority and influence. In the face of this collapse Mother Lucy Smith fled to Union Village. The visiting elders struggled to check the "libertine spirit," and some of the "sincere and thinking part" in the village became convinced of the need for "reform."[50]

As the "better part" at Pleasant Hill began to gain control over the "mischief makers," according to Youngs, the apostates secured the passage of a law against the society. On February 11, 1828, the General Assembly of the Commonwealth of Kentucky approved "An Act to Regulate Civil Proceedings Against Certain Communities having Property in Common." The Believers responded with a publication edited by Richard McNemar defending the social and economic arrangements of the Shakers. Although the ultimate outcome of the controversy and conflict remained uncertain at the time he was writing, Youngs made it clear that the cost of these affairs to the society in the West had been considerable. All of the western villages, but especially Pleasant Hill, had suffered much on account of the "*false* believers." Quite likely the cost to William S. Byrd was also great, for he was experiencing increasingly poor health during these months of confusion.[51]

BEARING THE CROSS

William S. Byrd's letters to his father form an instructive commentary upon the theological issues which attracted the Byrds to the United Society of Believers. The letters also serve as an indication of his growing capacity to articulate the ideas which he found central to his new religious position. In the letters themselves there is evidence of William's developing desire to address himself to religious issues. The theological sections of the letters constitute a synopsis of the most important concerns for the Shakers during the early decades of the nineteenth century. In fact, William's letters provide an unsystematic but quite sophisticated statement of Shaker theology. They echo themes struck by leading Shaker theologians in the West with whom he was personally acquainted, including Richard McNemar, Benjamin S. Youngs, and John Dunlavy. Byrd took "very great satisfaction" in observing that his views on "subjects of importance" coincided with those of the leaders.[52]

The heart of Shaker theology for William Byrd lay in the unique claim concerning the person and work of the founder of the society, Mother Ann Lee. The Believers affirmed that "the same Christ that dwelt in Jesus of Nazareth" had made a second appearance in Ann Lee of Manchester, England, who was thus "the spiritual Mother of all the new creation of God." That same spirit was now present in Christ's people, the members of the United Society of Believers, who were set apart from the world and therefore stood as a living judgment upon the creatures of the world. The Believers, wrote William, are destined to enjoy "that peace and happiness which passeth all understanding." Likewise those in union with Christ possess the power of God which enables them to endure and suffer all things for the sake of Christ and the Gospel.[53]

Byrd's view of Mother Ann Lee corresponds with the description provided by Benjamin S. Youngs in the *Testi-*

mony. Youngs pointed to "the energy of the eternal Word" as the force responsible for salvation. By it Christ Jesus "overcame the spirit and power of human depravity, and was sanctified and set apart in the work of redemption, as the first-born in the new creation." In the same way, he wrote, "it was by the revelation of Christ, and the energy of that same eternal Word . . . that the woman was taken out of, and separated from her correspondent relation to the fallen state of man, and made a spiritual woman." The church, in turn, which is to be "separated from the unclean," needs "both a father and a mother," which they find in Christ Jesus and Ann Lee. Youngs wrote, "Therefore, as there was a natural Adam and Eve, who were the first foundation pillars of the world, and the first joint-parentage of the human race; so there is also a spiritual Adam and Eve, who are the first foundation pillars of the Church, and the first joint-parentage of all the children of redemption. And as the world, truly and properly, proceedeth from Father and Mother, in the line of generation; so the Church, truly and properly, proceedeth from Father and Mother in the line of regeneration." Thus the regenerate order rests upon a proper understanding of the "foundation pillars" of the church.[54]

The "true church," in the words of John Dunlavy, "is the temple of God, and that temple is holy." It is comprised of the Believers "who have gained power over all sin." "For myself," affirmed Byrd, "I believe that Gods object in creating man was to make him honourable, and happy, and thereby promote his own glory, and that although he became lost from him by disobedience that he has provided a way whereby all souls may be saved that will come down and submit to it." According to the Shakers, God's plan of salvation required that the Believers suffer all things in order to obtain "full power over sin." Ann Lee proclaimed that the fundamental nature of sin was lust and that all activity associated with sexual impulses was evil. Therefore it was necessary for Believers to "live after the spirit, and not after the flesh." The Shakers were to mortify the flesh and thereby to "bear the cross," eschewing all sexual intentions and associations as well as all institutions related directly to the sexual patterns of the world, including marriage and the natural family.[55]

William S. Byrd and his fellow Shakers (including his father Charles) wrestled daily with the principle of the cross. The practice of celibacy proved difficult for many Believers, but Shaker theologians did not equivocate on the principle. Dunlavy wrote, "Those who follow Christ, follow him, not in the generation, but in the regeneration." He stated plainly that "marrying or living in the works thereof is inconsistent with the life of the true followers of Christ." Almost two years after taking up residence at Pleasant Hill, William acknowledged to his father that he was still not in possession of "that state of felicity which is in reserve for the righteous." On the contrary, he noted, his life was one of "daily suffering" which included both "mental and bodily affliction." Charles's struggle with the principle of bearing the cross was even more anguishing in view of his concern for family and spouse. His diaries show the pain of his reflections. "The doctrine of our Saviour which they [the Believers] alone practise, the crucifying of the old man in the tenderest point, bring a sword and not peace, in families where a part and not the whole number join the Believers." Later he noted, "A married couple who decline and disregard the happiness enjoyed by Believers as a sister and a brother are like the dog in Asops fable, who threw away the substance and caught at the shadow."[56]

The Byrds were not alone in their struggle with the flesh. William reported that the apostasy of 1827 involved an especially large percentage of young members of the society, many of whom married immediately after leaving the village. James and Lucy Gass, prominent and respected Shaker leaders, gave up the struggle and returned to the marital pattern of the world. Even some who stayed in the community were not always able to control the flesh. Leonard Jones, William's close friend, was disciplined by the leaders for "molesting" some of the young female members of the society, allegedly in order to test their commitment to Shakerism. William was ashamed of Jones's behavior, but by his own admission he himself was not immune to the sexual impulses of a post-adolescent male. Bearing the cross remained for him a continual struggle.[57]

The Believers who wished to live free of sin were to lead "a life of daily selfdenial and abstainance from every thing that defileth," in William's words. Thus celibacy was not the only requirement of the Shakers. The Believers were to forsake all aspects of worldly existence, including the holding of private property. John Dunlavy stated that this principle of "the true order of the gospel" requires a Believer to renounce the "former selfish disposition and claim in *heart and practice*, with all the gratifications pertaining to said claim," and to come into "a joint union, in which what is possessed by an individual, is possessed by the whole, so that a just and impartial equality reigns among the whole, and the rich and the poor share an equal and universal privilege." In this way, he wrote, "the church and people of God are united in one body and one Spirit and have all things common, a common interest and common inheritance in all good things, whether temporal or spiritual."[58]

The Shaker principle of "joint interest" explains William's unending drive to acquire property in order that he might transfer it to the society. He recognized that his own natural instincts were acquisitive and that those who took literally the biblical injunction to forsake all could not be content merely to wean their affections "mentally" from such things. Christ's own example was clear, he noted. Therefore "we ought in obedience to the command of Christ, to give up all that we have." The concept of communal property was at the heart of the difficulty Charles Byrd experienced with the Believers. His reluctance to surrender control of his possessions reflects his background.

The public recognition and achievements of the Byrd family ultimately rested on the possession of private property and the influence derived from it.[59]

As a corollary to the ideal of not owning property, the Believers were expected to labor for their part of the community's resources. Individual needs were met by the society, but everyone was expected to contribute to the joint interest through manual labor. The issue of manual labor was not merely a matter of community responsibility, but also a religious principle extending back to the teachings of Mother Ann Lee. Benjamin S. Youngs articulated the idea as follows: "As all the members of the Church are equally holden, according to their abilities, to maintain and support one joint-interest, in union and conformity to the order and government of the Church; therefore, all labour with their hands, to maintain the mutual comfort and benefit of one another by honest industry and acts of kindness—not by compulsion, but of choice, from a principle of faith, justice and equality." William Byrd regarded this community injunction as especially conducive to good health, and for that reason urged his father to follow Shaker practice too. That counsel caused Charles considerable anxiety, for he was unaccustomed to physical labor.[60]

Forsaking all for the gospel also involved the sacrifice of one's own will to that of the United Society of Believers as expressed by the ministry. The elders and eldresses spoke for the heavenly parentage and for all members of the resurrection order. Thus was unity with God and with fellow Believers established. Union was the ultimate objective of the community. Those living in unity with the spirit of Christ will reflect harmony with one another in their daily intercourse. The Shakers recognized, however, that the ideal and the reality did not always coincide. Thus the turmoil at Pleasant Hill in the 1820s was a scandal to the fundamental principles of the society and potentially a stumbling block to new converts such as the Byrds. The troublesome events during William Byrd's residence at Shakertown proved the difficulty of reaching high ideals, but they did nothing, in his eyes, to tarnish the vision informing those principles.[61]

DEATH AND ITS AFTERMATH

William S. Byrd wrote his last letter to his father on July 14, 1828. It was preoccupied with the same issue that had been on his mind in his initial letter of June 22, 1826, the financial arrangements made for the purchase of the McMurtry farm. Charles had expressed growing fears about the safety of his investment. William displayed some fresh impatience with his father, but then apologized for liberties he had taken with him, recollecting that Charles had never been totally pleased with the venture. On August 25 Charles Byrd died suddenly. No evidence is available concerning the immediate cause of his death. According to the most reliable account, the Judge became ill during a session of court and died within a few days. The official records at Pleasant Hill contain the following brief entry. "Byrd, Charles Wylling—born July, 1770. Nativity, Westover, Charles City Co. Va. Believed in 1826. Was associate Judge of the federal Court in Ohio at his decease, which office he had filled about twenty years or upwards. He had purchased land adjoining this Society, and was preparing to remove here when he died suddenly Aug. 25. 1828." At the time of his death the Judge was discussing a proposal for resigning his position, moving to Pleasant Hill, and building some appropriate housing for his family. He had even suggested a possible trade of his home in Sinking Spring for a farm adjacent to Shakertown. Earlier, in the spring, he had stated that, apart from his family responsibilities, he was "willing to give up all for Christ" and that he had "unlimited confidence in the Believers."[62]

It is impossible to determine precisely the full impact of Charles's sudden death upon his son. Earlier William had written of making his own peace with the prospect of death, stating that he did not fear "an early dissolution from bodily indisposition." He and his father had had a very close relationship, in part because of the contrast between himself and Powel and also because he and his father shared the same faith. Charles's death was probably a great shock to him. During the summer of 1828 William himself was experiencing very poor health. It is uncertain whether his physical problems were compounded by the news of his father's death, but it appears that he was unable to be present for the funeral in Sinking Spring. Later, in mid-September, William traveled to Ohio for a period of approximately two weeks. Francis Voris may have accompanied him on the trip. William received a small inheritance from his father's estate, including four acres of land in Adams County, Ohio, a tract originally acquired by Charles from his father's estate.[63]

The events of the next five months are equally difficult to establish. William's health apparently went from bad to worse. The restraint which the Judge may have exercised upon the Shaker leadership at Pleasant Hill was no longer operative after his death. Perhaps because of new pressures by the Believers and because of his own perception of his worsening physical condition, William wrote his last will and testament on November 4, 1828, a document witnessed by three Shakers, including his long-term friend, Leonard Jones. In the will, William bequeathed all of his possessions, including most notably half of the McMurtry acreage, to Abram Wilhite and Francis Voris, trustees of the village, "for the use and benefit of the Society of people called Shakers, at Pleasant Hill." In addition, he itemized other assets to be given to the village: stocks, cash, and his portion of a family of slaves held by David Meade. He also gave to the trustees the "power to emancipate" any of the slaves who came into their hands through him. If ever there had been any doubt about Byrd's willingness to forsake all for the cause of the gospel, his last will and testament set that to rest. The community formally acknowledged his action in the church records at Pleasant Hill. "Nov. 4th, 1828 William S. Byrd made a will in which he devised all his property and estate to Abram Wilhite and Francis Voris Trustees, in which was included his undivided moiety of a tract of land lying on Cedar Run about a mile south of the village."[64]

Two and a half months after signing the will, William S. Byrd was dead, the precise cause of his death unknown. The ministry at Pleasant Hill took brief notice of his demise in a letter to New Lebanon written several months later: "There are three who have put off their earthly bodys in this place, since our last communications to you. viz Charit Montport depart this life Dec'r 6th 1828. William S. Byrd Jan'y 19th 1829. Genny Vancleave, March 21st." The official biographical register of Pleasant Hill has a brief entry directly following the notice of Charles Byrd: "Byrd, William S.—born perhaps in 1806. Nativity, perhaps Jessamine Co. Ky. Believed and removed from Ohio to P. H. Ky. in 1826, and removed from the Junior Order into the Chh. the same fall. Deceased Jan. 19, 1829." Thus was concluded the short life of this young Shaker.[65]

In fact, however, these were not the last references to William S. Byrd in either the formal or the informal records of the community. The official journal of the church took note almost six years later of the final resolution of William's will by entering the record of a deed drawn on October 1, 1834, giving title to 110 acres of land on Cedar Run to the trustees of the village. These acres were William's portion of the tract purchased jointly with his father. The same manuscript documents the purchase by the Shakers on January 21, 1846, of 138 acres from Samuel O. Byrd and Jane W. Long, the children of Charles who inherited his portion of the McMurtry property.[66]

In 1838, almost ten years after William's death, during the period of Shaker history known as "Mother Ann's Work" or the "Era of Manifestations"—a period of revival within the society—special and pointed reference was made to "William Bird" in a vision received by Sarah Pool on September 17, 1838. Pool, a Believer who came to Pleasant Hill as a child in 1808, was the first medium to receive a spirit vision during the revival era at Shakertown. Her vision addressed a question about which there remains considerable ambiguity, namely, whether William was ever formally received into the Church, the inner circle of the Shakers.[67]

According to the written account of the vision, Sarah Pool fell into a trance and traveled to a remote city having walls "which seemed to be composed of no earthly materials: its appearance was that of pure white." At her approach, the gate opened and she entered the city. She continued, "I beheld an innumerable band of *spiritual beings* marching toward us; the brethren being to the right hand, and the sisters to my left. They sang a song saying, Come view, come view this beautiful city; where the wicked cease from troubling, and the weary souls find rest. This song was accompanied by an appropriate motion of bowing and rising, which somewhat resembled the undulations of a field of wheat, when gently put in motion by a gale of wind. As the company drew near, I discovered the front ranks to be composed of all the believers who had died in the church order, at Pleasant Hill, with two or three exceptions as I afterwards learned, and one of these, that is, William Bird, has since appeared to me in a *dream*, and said, that as I had passed him by unnoticed at that time, he was then come to let me know that he yet belonged to that order." William Byrd was both a participant in Pool's vision and the subject of her dream. These records suggest the tenacity of the collective memory of the Shaker community at Pleasant Hill. They also hint at the potential impact of Byrd's presence upon the village.[68]

Even these visionary appearances were not the end of the story of William S. Byrd. Nearly two years later on July 29, 1840, a spirit letter *from Byrd* was received by Katherine McCullough, an inspired "instrument" or medium at Pleasant Hill who had become a Believer in 1833. The letter was addressed to Martin Runyon, a member of the community who had served for several years as a deacon in the church and as a trustee. Runyon appears to have been a friend of Byrd during his residence at the community and perhaps attended him during his final illness. McCullough was a young child when Byrd was at Shakertown. On the one hand, this spirit letter is typical of hundreds received by Shakers during the revival period. Spirit letters possessed certain identifiable marks, including stylized descriptions of messages and gifts from former leaders of the society. On the other hand, this particular letter includes certain details bearing a striking resemblance to those of Byrd's biography. It was an epistle of encouragement to Runyon drawing upon Byrd's own experiences.[69]

The spirit letter corroborates the picture of William Byrd which emerges from the letters to his father. Among the Shakers, William had a reputation as a letter-writer. The opening lines confirm the same. Byrd's spirit writes, "In union with our blessed Mother, I now have this opportunity to converse with you by way of letter. It is a great and glorious privilege, one that I prize more than all earthly enjoyments." The spirit letter confirmed other aspects of Byrd's biography too. Byrd's spirit said that he was "called by the sounding trumpet of God . . . to give up all earthly enjoyments for my salvation." Furthermore, the letter described Byrd during his lifetime as "a falling leaf, or fading flower, that bloomed to last but a short time." In the spirit letter Byrd also thanked Martin Runyon for his "unwearied pains during my illness," making it likely that Runyon took care of Byrd during his last days of life.[70]

The references to Byrd's biography support the principal objective of the spirit letter, namely, to encourage Martin Runyon in his own struggle to bear the cross. The letter makes this explicit when it states, "Now beloved brother, precious Mother says, you have waded through deep tribulation, you have suffered and toiled for your salvation. You forsook your house and land, your wife, and children for my sake, and the kingdom of heaven, saith the Lord, and great will be your reward in the kingdom, if ye will persevere, and hold out to the end; for I say unto you, there is none that enters the kingdom, only by the cross of Christ: it is none, saith the Lord, but these who are willing to give up all, the world, flesh and devil, who are willing to bow low, low, and humble themselves in true submission, before the Lord God, and his heavenly train." As a seal of this promise and as further encouragement, Martin Runyon was given "a golden box filled with the true substance of the gospel" from Mother Ann and "a twig of the great union tree" filled with "little birds" from Father William, Mother Ann Lee's brother. Byrd's spirit closes the letter on a note of love and humility. He writes, "Now I will draw to a close, by sending you my kind love and blessing, in twelve low bows, to the Ministry, Elders, brethren and sisters. So fare ye well with my kind and everlasting love."[71]

CONCLUSIONS

It is no longer puzzling why William S. Byrd chose to join the Shakers and live at Pleasant Hill. The United Society of Believers and Shakertown had much to offer him. Byrd responded positively to the Shaker challenge to bear the cross. He was drawn by the radical vision of a society of Believers united in pursuit of full salvation. The concept of living in a regenerate order without sin proved inviting. Additionally, he saw the Shakers as a legitimate family, its members bound to one another by love. Fully aware of the fragility of familial relationships in the natural world, Byrd desired to be part of a spiritual family with a heavenly parentage. Furthermore, his natural father approved of his actions and joined him in principle if not in practice.

William Byrd knew chronic disability and discomfort at

first hand. The preoccupation of the Shakers with health, diet, manual labor, and the wholesome life was therefore compelling. He had witnessed at second hand the difficulties confronting young professionals and the despair which drove his brother to suicide. He found an answer to those potential dilemmas in the role of correspondent and apologist for the Shaker community, an attractive and potentially prestigious position among the Believers. Byrd enjoyed the attention of the leaders of the community and the admiration which his skills brought from his fellow Believers. His father's unending anxieties and complaints about financial misfortunes made the Shaker principle of joint interest very enticing, particularly if he was in a position to bring substantial resources with him into the church. From that point on his needs would be met by the society. Finally—and not insignificantly—the society provided a seemingly endless number of friends to encourage and support him, to raise his spirit when he was gripped by melancholy, and to care for him when he was sick.

Deprivation theory is useful in the case of Byrd, but only if it is not limited to socioeconomic issues and if it is not applied dogmatically. However well the Shakers succeeded in meeting his conscious and unconscious needs, the record is clear that the situation among the Believers was far from perfect, particularly during the years of Byrd's residency at Pleasant Hill. In fact, the society added to his problems in a number of ways. William discovered that the flesh prevailed over the spirit among many in the community. Instead of harmony there was discord; family relationships among the Shakers could be bitter and vile as well as loving. Rebellion and insurrection against the leaders of the community who represented the spiritual parentage reminded William of the situation in his own natural family. The principle of joint interest had its problems too, for there were those who wished to destroy the security of the community by apostatizing and removing their shares.[72]

Even the principle of the cross was not above attack and subversion by Shaker leaders and members alike. Byrd knew well the struggle associated with that principle, a struggle which added to his periods of depression and possibly to his physical pain. Not even in his chosen role of letter-writer or apologist could he gloss over the harsh realities of life among the Shakers at Pleasant Hill. Nevertheless, he refused to be discouraged by the problems plaguing the resurrection order. He had become a true believer and therefore was willing to try to overcome the dissonance between the heavenly vision and earthly realities. He lived his short life as a Believer confident that Christ's second appearing in Ann Lee had inaugurated a new age.

Fortified by that conviction, William Byrd had much to offer the Shakers at Pleasant Hill. He brought to the village his name and the "honourable standing" associated with it. He had skills at his command which were sorely needed in that particular time. His financial resources were substantial and useful for the community. His enthusiasm for the cause of Christ and the gospel provided a valuable antidote to the insurrection and apostasy of others. But the early and premature end to his life cut short his potential contributions to the society and the community. The Shaker legacy of William S. Byrd includes both tangibles and intangibles: a tract of land and other physical resources, a place in the collective experience and memory of the community, and a collection of very revealing letters which document his efforts to bear the cross during tumultuous times at Pleasant Hill.[73]

EDITORIAL PROCEDURES

The texts of William S. Byrd's letters to his father are drawn from the original manuscripts included in the collection of Byrd Papers at the Lilly Library at Indiana University, Bloomington. The editorial conventions governing the preparation of the letters for publication include the following. The texts stand as Byrd wrote them. His punctuation and spelling, with few exceptions, have been retained. Obvious slips of the pen have been corrected silently. Double punctuation, which occurs in a few locations, has been reduced to single conventional patterns. In a few places dashes have been replaced with appropriate punctuation marks and periods have been inserted. The use of quotation marks has been made consistent. Editorial insertions in the text are identified by the use of square brackets [ ]. Editorial conjectures are indicated by the use of braces { }. The same conventions are employed in the editing of the appendixes. Annotation of the letters and of the documents in the appendixes has been largely confined to the identification of proper names and to the explication of items of special importance or difficulty. Several personal references have remained elusive. The manuscripts are in excellent condition, and therefore relatively few problems are identified in the notes.[74]

The Letters of
WILLIAM S. BYRD
—— *to* ——
CHARLES
WILLING
BYRD

Dear Papa,

I arrived here safe last friday afternoon. As I passed through Lexington I made some further enquery about our Bank stock. I saw Mr. Morton[1] and Mr. Legrand[2] together, and was informed by the latter that it would be impracticable for me to negotiate a sale of my stock on advantageous terms, but thought that he could sell it for at least six hundred dollars, and promised to let me know very soon the most it would sell for. In the mean time one of the Believers, Francis Voorheese [Voris], undertook to negotiate the sale of the stock, and is now about to confirm a contract with a gentleman in Lexington. He is to receive for my seventeen shares, one thousand and twenty dollars, in specie, or its value in Lexington of commonwealth notes, which he thinks he can exchange for a larger sum on this side of the River. If you will send me a power of attorney I will get the favor of Frances Voorheese, to sell Evelyns[3] for me likewise. He says for both, he can get seventeen hundred dollars in specie, and if you could without any inconvenience transfer to me five of your shares, Frances will then purchase for me McMurtrys place[4] one mile south of the Village. He considers it to be a very valuable property, and thinks that it would be the very best disposition that I could possibly make of all the money that I can command to purchase it. The title Francis says is indisputable, perfectly safe, and I can depend upon him. He transacts the most important business for the Society, and appears to be well acquainted with land titles, and all kind of business. Should you wish it he is willing to sell for you the whole of your stock on the same terms on which he will sell mine. He thinks there will be no difficulty in disposing of it all. It is my determination in case you will give me a power of attorney to sell Evelyns, to transfer to her my dismal swamp interest, which is likely to become much more valuable than it has been. Should you transfer five shares of your stock to me, I suppose a power of attorney would be necessary for that also.

If you can assist me in this way without frustrating your plans in any way I will be much obliged to you. I did not call at Chaumiere, but saw Deans wife[5] in Lexington, and learned from her that the family were all well but Uncle Kidder,[6] and that he had gone off, a few days before with Sampson[7] and the carriage, and that they had not been heard of since. I have suffered with costifness more than usual for some days past, but am somewhat better now. I have not yet been able to get any more information about the place at the mill,[8] the dam, though I believe is south of the dwelling house. It is however I understand a very healthy place. I remain Dear papa very Affectionately,

William S Byrd

P.S. I will thank you to send the certificates with your name indorsed on the back of each, as Evelyns Guardian, and also a check for her dividends now due three hundred and thirty dollars. In case you send a power of attorney to sell five shares of yours I will thank you likewise to transmit a check for the dividends, one hundred and fifty dollars on the same.

Least you may overlook some technicalty I have inclosed you something like a blank form of a power of attorney and check for Evelyns.

If you send your certificates for five shares it will be necessary as I understand for you to sign your name on the back of each.

Whenever I feel disposed to do any thing, I have access to a room where I can employ myself I believe very usefully without any injury I suppose resulting from it, I do not confine myself to that exercise alone but walk about occasionally. It is an easy business but as you do not know any thing about it I will not undertake to explain it.

Pleasant Hill, July 13th, 1826

My Dear Father,

I received your letter last Saturday evening. It was my intention before you made the request to write to you frequently, believing that it would be agreeable to you to hear from myself, and the Society of which I am a member, very often.

John Dunleavy[9] is absent at this time, and I am therefore unable to say what course he would advise me to pursue either about medicine, or change of residence. But it appears to be the decided opinion of Francis Voris, that the water of this place is more strongly impregnated with lime than the water at Union Village, and Mr. Turner, whom I will call Elder Samuel, told me that If I wished to go to Union Village, the Believers would not object to it, but at the same time observed to me, that after having resided a number of years at both places, he was well satisfyed that Pleasant Hill, was in all respects the most healthy. You will I suppose receive a letter from brother Frances, on this subject, and I therefore will not write so fully as I otherwise might have done. If after the perusal of our letters, you think you can comply with the request made in my last without any inconvenience to yourself, and without any injury to the rest of your family, I will be much pleased. I should be very sorry to go contrary to your advice in any thing, although I have arrived to that time of life when by the laws of our Country the empire of the Father, or other Guardian, gives place to the empire of reason. And I do therefore hope that after you have read both of our letters you will think differently upon the subject, and be disposed to excuse me for repeating the request made in my last communication.

I have been living almost ever since my return to this place in a framed building, answering to the East house at Union Village, on this side of the town, which is I believe called the Church. For some time past I have been engaged in the perusal of Dunleavy's Manifesto. I do not however confine myself to reading, or any particular business, but employ myself as much as I can in the fresh air when the weather will permit. I am glad to be able to infer from what you said in your letter, that you have already derived some advantage from a little manual labour, and do cherish the hope, notwithstanding your age and bodily infirmities, that it may prove a lasting benefit to your health. Flax seed oil has been very highly recommended to me for the removal of costifness. I procured some the other day, and although I have not yet derived much benefit from the use of it, I entertain the hope that by increasing the dose as I did this morning, it may prove more efficacious. But if upon a farther trial I do not obtain much relief from it, for fear of suffering too much from experiments, I will return to the use of the root of rhubarb, or to the blue pill,[10] as you advised, or perhaps both, and trust that by increasing the quantity of the former, even though I should not take the latter atall, that it may be attended with its former salutary effects.

I met Patrick[11] the other day out in the road on his way I believe from the Green River Country, to Jessamine. That I suppose must have been the Texas[12] to which he alluded in his conversation with Nathaniel Massie. I wrote a letter to Molly the other day in which I enclosed your memorandum, which I think you directed me to place in Evelyns hands. I have not yet sent the letter, being desirous if practicable to obtain a private conveyance, in order to get a coupple of shirts which I suppose must be finished by this time, as the muslin was placed in safe hands in Lexington to be sent out to Chaumiere. Should you see Mr. Burgess I will thank you to re[me]mber me to him in terms of affection, indeed I would not object to your shewing him this letter although written in a careless style. I feel very much obliged to him for the anxiety which he has at all times manifested for our welfare, and will take a pleasure in receiving from him from time, to time, any communication which he may think proper to make to me.

I suppose you still have it in view to visit this place in September. The Believers, will I have no doubt as well as myself, be very glad to see you. Many of them have expressed to me their desire to form an acquaintance with you. As brother Leonard wishes to address you, I will now conclude my letter. Remember me if you please to all the family, and believe me to be

Your Very Affectionate Son,
William S Byrd

P.S. Elder Samuel desired me to tell you, that he was thankful to you for your letter to him of which I was the bearer.

Pleasant Hill, November 28th, 1826

Dear Papa,

Not having received any letter from Evelyn since I left her, I am still unable to inform you whether Aunt Woodson[13] ever got yours, which was written soon after your return home. But Evelyns silence induces me to believe that she never did, as I requested her in case the letter was received, to let me know it immideately, in order that I might answer your enquery. Elder Samuel Turner, upon hearing your letter read, told me that he had never given Joseph Reynolds[14] any such information as he stated to you, and was particularly desirous that I should write and let you know it, that he knew of a number that had not only obtained full power over all sin, but were actually out of the flesh, though in the body, born again. For myself, I can discern a great difference between being regenerated, and just merely living without sin, indeed I believe it is in the power of some, to live in this world without committing sin, and that they may do so merely from fear, without having any religion, and that if it was not for the apprehension of future punishment would be the same old creatures that they were before they made any profession of religion. Of this however I am not very positive, but at the same time I am confident that when we are born of God we will know that we are resurrected, and serve him through love, and not from fear, and delight in knowing and doing his will. I have been engaged for some time past in reading the new Testament, {that} is I spend a short time almost every day in that way, but {do not} confine myself to that kind of reading, and although I have read over and over the whole bible, yet I cannot say that I ever took any pleasure in the perusal of it before.

Frances procured for me a buroe, to keep my cloathes, and other things in. It was not quite finished when he bought it, although it had been made some time before. I suppose alltogether it will not cost me more than eleven dollars. It is a very handsome one, and I understand from him that if it had been bought out of town, it would have come to about twenty two. I found it necessary likewise to get a {new} stove into my room, as I could not read with any satisfaction in the publick part of the house, and it is not always agreeable to me as you know to be in company. I am as you may suppose affraid of some injury resulting from it, but I am in hopes it will not be so great as it would be if I had not the privilege of regulating it as I please. I do a little manual labour about the house, and stables, and walk, and ride, occasionally, the former every day, and the latter which is I believe the best exercise that {we can} take, not unfrequently. Our good brother John Shane,[15] desired me to tell you that they were all pleased with me here, and told me that I must mention him in particular. I now take two meals in the day, one in the morning, and one in the evening, instead of three, and I think it is a great advantage to me, as my stomach has more time to digest the food. I feel disposed to say a few words to you about Evelyns cloathing. I do not pretend to dictate to you the proper course to pursue with her, but it appears to me and I hope you will not be dissatisfyed with me for saying so, that you ought not to wish to punish her, by withholding from her, the means of cloathing herself as formerly, on account of her late conduct towards you, as it was just such as you might have expected after embracing the faith of this Society. And further if you think the life she now leads is calculated to bring destruction upon her, after, you surely ought not to wish to render her {life in} this present world, less agreeable. Molly told me that she would have visited you while you were at this place if it had been in her power, and that you could not have sent to her children a more acceptable present than you did. Benjamin S Youngs, the Author of the Testimony, is here at this time. The Society have gotten several new modes of worshipping in the dance[16] from the Eastward, which are very beauti-full, far more so than any that was practised while you were here.

The work in which I am engaged, that is to put to death my own self, is as I mentioned in my last letter a great work, but difficult as it is, I suppose it would be more so were I in the enjoyment of good mental and bodily health, and I think it not unlikely that it is the same way with yourself. I believe {that} from my acquaintance with you that you would in [this] situation, bear the cross of Christ better than myself. I ought not to be so but I do not think I can help it.

P   I will thank you to let me know if you can the month when our Virginia dividends, become due. Tucker Wood-son[17] I understand has commenced the practice of the law and is in partnership with his father,

Your Affectionate Son,
William S Byrd

When will your court be in session.

The Post {is} here, and we {will send} letters by him to Nicholasville[18] where they {are} mailed, but Harrodsburgh is the place for you {to send} your letters.

Pleasant Hill, December 29th, 1826

Dear Papa,

I received your last letter of the 25th ultimo, at the time I suppose when mine to you was on the road. I was very much concerned to hear of your late indisposition, and feel somewhat apprehensive that a continuation of it has prevented you from answering my letter, as a longer time has elapsed without your writing than is usual after the receipt of my communications.

As you observed in your letter, it is a very great satisfaction to me to reflect that my conduct is acceptable to yourself, and to the good believers, and I can say with truth, that from my earliest infancy to the present time, I have allways valued your favour, far more than any of the good things that ever have resulted from it, and was never able to enjoy any peace of mind when I had reason to believe that you were displeased with me. It is highly gratifying to me moreover to know, that while I am doing that which I believe to be the will of my heavenly father, that my conduct meets the approbation of my earthly parent. Although no important change has taken place in me, I do humbly hope, and confidently believe, that I shall always have resolution to do that which my conscience tells me is right, however contrary it may be to my inclination, and that I never will refuse to make any sacrifice, that my faith may lead me to make, for christs sake and the Gospels, even though I should not receive the promised reward. But perhaps I am wrong in writing thus, as it looks too much like calling into question the truth of that God, who has promised every thing to those who have forsaken all, for his sake. I have not made any legal transfer of my property, I am speaking now particularly of the farm which we hold between us, but what I did do with your concurrence, which was to give Francis the privilege of cultivating it without accounting for the profits, amounts in substance to pretty much the same thing. And I do not know but that if the half of the place belonged to the Society instead of yourself, that is if they had paid the ballance for it I would make a transfer of that, and all that I have, to the community, as you advised me to do when you were with me, and then I believe I would feel still more comfortable in my situation, and more like one of the body. The recollection of having forced you as it were to pay for the above mentioned tract of land, at a time when it was particularly inconvenient, wounds my feelings.[19] I do nevertheless indulge the hope that in the end it may not prove a serious injury to yourself or any of the family.

Henry Miller[20] is at this time in the state of Indianna,[21] where he will probably remain until the spring. Francis Voris accompanied him there, and is not expected home this season. The former desired me to give you this information, and likewise to present to yourself and family his best love. I have experienced some inconvenience from the unexpected, and long absence of Francis, not being able to procure leggons, which are so necessary at this time of the year, and a few other little articles, and consequently have to go without riding almost altogether. Should I at any time make a legal transfer of myself and all the little I have to the Society, I will make known my wants freely to those whose province it will be to supply them, and at the same time, tell them, that if I ask for any thing that in their opinion is not necessary for me to have, to let me know it with as little ceremony. If I was governed by my own natural feelings I would make a very different disposition of myself and property, but now that I profess to follow Christ, to live after the spirit, and not after the flesh, it would be highly inconsistent with my profession I suppose, if we take the words of our Saviour litterally, to act differently. The professors of religion through the world maintain that we are not required to forsake all litterally, but only mentally as they call it, that is I suppose, that we should not place all our affections on temporal things. And notwithstanding the express words of Christ, there are so many figurative expressions in the bible, and seeming contradictions, that it would look like presumption in us to contradict them if our Saviour had not set us the example, and commanded us to follow him. This appears to place the thing beyond a doubt. I do therefore suppose that we ought in obedience to the command of Christ, to give up all that we have, and follow him when there is no serious obstacles in the way.

I have not received any letters from Chaumiere since I left there. The Society I believe in general enjoy good health. I was pleased to hear of Powels disposition to do something for himself,[22] and do suppose that he may in the way you mentioned make a livelyhood. Enquires are frequently made of me about the time of your return here. I suppose you still calculate as you did when with us, of coming again in the spring of the year. Give my love if you please to the family. When Francis is at home he allways wishes to read your letters to me. I remain

Your Affectionate Son,
William S Byrd

Pleasant Hill, January 25th, 1827

Dear Papa,

I received your letter of the ninth instant. It was just such a one as I wanted to get from you. Soon after I wrote to you, I communicated to Elder Samuel, my feelings towards the Believers, and indeavoured to find out from him, whether it would be agreeable to them, at this time to ad-

mit me into the Church as one of the body. He told me that
he could not give me a decisive answer until he consulted
his companions in the ministry on the subject, but that his
impression then was it would not be proper for them to do
so at this time. Our ministry accordingly took the thing
into consideration, and afterwards communicated to me
the result, which was, that it would not be proper for me
at this time to sign their covenant, not because they supposed I was deficient in understanding or faith, but merely
on account of strangers, who might suppose I had been
taken in unawares, not having had time sufficient to satisfy
my mind on the subject. They assured me however at the
same time as Elder Samuel had done the day before, that
they would all view me as nearly related to them, and as
much one of the body, as if I had actually signed the compact.

I am aware that no precaution can be taken to obviate
altogether the diliterious effects of the stove.[23] But I am
satisfyed from experience that the injury resulting from it
may be much lessoned by keeping a vessel of water upon
it. Until I made the experiment, I had no idea that it would
make any material difference, but as soon as I placed the
vessel of water upon the stove I noticed a most important
change in the air, and likewise when I left the room, I did
not feel the cold as sensibly as before.

Your letter to Francis was received at the same time that
mine was taken out of the Office. The ministry, as well as
himself, almost always express a desire to see your letters
to me, when they know that I have received them, and Elder Samuel desired me to tell you, that if at any time there
should be any thing, that you would not like to be communicated to any one but myself, to give me a hint of it
that it may not be read. For myself I scarcely know what
to say about it, but feel most disposed to leave you to ex-

ercise your own judgment on the occasion. Mother Lucy's parents are still alive, and have been I believe for some years past, members of the Society in the State of New York. They are wealthy people. All this you may have heard before, but it is new to me, and I therefore thought I would communicate it to you. Leonard has received your letter, and is I believe about to answer it. He will probably give you some account of his late vision, and if he was not such a visionary character, I should be more disposed than I am to think there was some meaning in it. Agreeable to your advice I addressed a letter to William Page,[24] which I suppose will reach him before he leaves Richmond, as I lost no time in writing after the receipt of your favour. I am very thankfull to you for your kind offer, but was able to procure the article I was most in want of with the ballance of the money you left with me. I have just received a letter from brother Francis. He was in good health, and desired me to present his love to you and to Hannah, as he calls your companion. Remember me to her if you please, and to all the family. That spirit of kindness, and humility, which she manifests towards you surely proceeds from a good source, and will I have no doubt receive its reward. Your message about the stove was delivered to me by brother Leonard. I will keep no fire in it when I can possibly do without, and when it is absolutely necessary, with as little as I can do with. I do not confine myself to the room, perhaps as much as you suppose, and it does not prevent me from going into company. Yours in love,

W S Byrd

PS. The ministry join me in love to you, to Mrs. Byrd, and to all the family, and Mother Lucy wishes to know, how Powel comes on with his goods. I had written a much longer letter to you, but not wishing to shew it to the ministry, as I told them, I abridged it considerably, but still I suppose this will be sufficient for this time. They all appear to be as anxious to hear my letters, as yours, when there is nothing that we would object to their knowing. They say they are interested in our wellfare and like to know, what is passing betwen us. I have answered the letter I received from Francis, and suppose he will return shortly, as Mother Lucy directed me to tell him that it was time for him to come home.

W S Byrd

This letter has been written some days. Uncle Woodson,[25] and his son Tucker, called upon me yesterday in a very friendly way, and gave me a kind invitation to visit them. This invitation was repeated by them both, with much apparent, and I have no doubt real sincerity, assuring me at the same time that they would allways make it a point of stopping, whenever they passed this way. Uncle Woodson observed while here, that he esteemed a conscientious shaker as much as any other man, and believed that his prospect for heaven was just as good. But I cannot give you an account of all that passed between us. Him and Tucker, appeared to be pretty much of the same mind on the subject, and both expressed their wish that I would visit them, and not be prevented on account of my profession, as they would all be as glad to see me as if I was a member of any other society. They had been absent from home about ten days. It was then supposed that Patrick would take Molly away somewhere. Evelyn had been for several weeks in Lexington.

Aunt Woodson received your letter.

Pleasant Hill, February 25th, 1827

Dear Papa,

Your favour of the tenth instant was received. On the same day I got one from Evelyn, acknowledging the receipt of a letter from myself, together with one which was enclosed to our friend Burgess, wherein I expressed to him my increasing confidence in Shakerism. Evelyns epistle was not much longer than usual, and as I do not know that the contents would be interesting to you I will forbear to communicate them. It was however written in a style more pleasing to me than any of her former letters. Henry Miller got home about the time I wrote to you, but I believe I omitted to mention his arrival. Francis has not yet returned, and no recent intelligence has been received about the Indiana Society. Had they been led by the counsel of the wise they never would have returned there, after being driven away by the army, but as it is I suppose they will now have to submit to the determination of those whose advice they heretofore rejected.[26]

Since you left us the Believers at this place sustained a pretty considerable loss by fire. Their blacksmith shop, together with several locust trees in front of it, was reduced to ashes. It has been since rebuilded, and the Society is now I hope notwithstanding the loss, increasing in all things. Our Sister Lucy[27] told me She was well pleased with the present of the peaches, as well as for the notice, and thankfull to you both. She desired me to present her love to you, and to Hannah, and the Bretheren and Sisters likewise. Brother John [Shain] received your letter. He had but a few moments before expressed to me his love for you in the warmest terms, and told me to remember him to you in love. He was very much pleased with the letter. Yours to brother Leonard has been received. He has lately changed his residence, and now lives at the griss Mill, with a family of old Believers, as they are some times called, to distinguish them from the young. Leonard was recently favoured with another vision, and will in all probability communicate it to you before a great while, as he is not at all disposed to keep any thing to himself that may in any way benefit others. Our Dr. Anthony Benezett,[28] has left us. The Author of the publication[29] you alluded to in your letter, was I suppose some professor of religion, and perhaps Office hunter, who was apprehensive that your example, and conversation, might have a pernicious effect upon Society, and probably pleased himself with the expectation of being able by argument, to induce you to resign your Office, and leave the Country. I was pleased to hear that you had not answered the publication, and well satisfyed with the reasons you assigned for not doing so.

There is nothing relating to yourself, or any member of your family, that would be uninteresting to me, and I therefore hope you will not fail to record in your next, the evidence that your little Samuel gave of his attachment to me. The Sisters frequently speak of him, and express their unfeigned anxiety to see him, as well as his parents. Your account of Jane was well calculated to excite a smile, as it did from the ministry, when I read it to them. They desired me to remember them all to you and to Hannah in love. James Congleton,[30] whose name it seems you have forgotten, as well as that of his acquaintance in Ohio, Edward Byrom,[31] told me to give to you his love, and I do suppose that if the Believers all knew that I was writing to you I would have more love messages to record, than the longest letter could contain.

I have just received a letter from William B. Page. The lastyears dividend which he deposited in the Bank of Richmond, was $28.77. I must now I believe conclude this letter, and remain in love

Your Son,
W. S Byrd

P.S. I have just received a letter from our acquaintance young Dr. Williamson[32] of Riply. It was as you may suppose written in a very friendly Style.

Agreeable to the request of William Page I acknowledged the receipt of his letter, as I did likewise of the dividends I received last summer, of I believe $184 and some cents, which I suppose was all correct. Mother [Lucy Smith] desired me to tell you that the first time we heard of poor Anthony after he left us, he was intoxicated.

The ministry express themselves to be altogether pleased with my manner of writing, as well as yours, and Elder Samuel told me that he thought I might do much good by writing. He was very well pleased with Dr. Williamsons letter to me, and requested me to invite him to pay us a visit. I have been conversing with Elder Samuel freely, as I have been allways incouraged to do, about my health, and the stove. He says he feels perfect union with me to get it out of my room, and substitute a kind of a fire place, more in the way of a Franklin stove. My room will then be not only far more healthy, but I can with less trouble make a fire in it. And besides all this I will then be able at all times to keep my feet dry, which I find to be absolutely necessary. Agreeable to Elder Samuel Turners request, I have just given Evelyn a particular invitation to visit the Believers. He says it would be pleasing to him for her to visit us, if he knew she would never become a member of the body.

W S Byrd

Pleasant Hill, April 11th, 1827

Dear father,

I received your favour of the 20th ultimo, just as I was about to visit my grand father Meades[33] and therefore postponed writing until my return. I had I believe within the last few months received several letters from Evelyn requesting me to visit them, and a few days previous to my going over a note was handed to me from Molly of the same character. The family were all well not excepting Molly herself, whom I expected to find in a very low state of health. Our Grand Mother told me that she had enjoyed better health this last season than the winter before, owing she said, to her resuming the practice of passing through the haul into the dining room to her meals, agreeable to your advice. Uncle Woodson is about to move to a place he has purchased by Frankfort. I found his wife at Chaumiere, where she expected to remain with a part of their family some weeks.

The Indianna Believers,[34] that is those of them that were expected here, have arrived, some having gone to other Societys. They are chiefly females. You wanted to know if any disposition had been made of their property left behind. I do not know certainly whether it was rented out or not, but I incline to think it was. Henry Miller returned with the Believers from West Union, but Frances has not got back, and I suppose it will be some days yet before he returns as he went to Union Village. Asuby[35] desired me to present her love to you, and told me that she had serious thoughts of paying you a visit at Sinking Spring, as she was anxious to see you and supposed that such a journey might benefit her health which is at this time very delicate. The ministry desire to be remembered to you, and likewise our Sister Charity,[36] who never fails to give her opinion of Charles when she receives a message of love, or at any time when occasion requires it. Anthony Benizett left us as I wrote you but before he got as far as Lexington determined that he would return. He was again received into the Society and in a few weeks went off, so that you will not be surprised to receive any kind of information about him. We have not heard from Leonard for some time and it is doubted by some whether he will ever return here again.

Davis Dunleavy, son of John Dunleavy deceased, recently had his backbone dislocated by a fall from a horse. Doctors were called in and soon pronounced him incurable, as they said it would be next to an impossibility to replace it. After they withdrew however, several of the bretheren determined that they would make an effort to replace it, which they did, and now although he is not out of danger I think he may recover.[37] I am not surprised at the unwillingness of your family to visit this place, as the life of the inhabitants is alltogether contrary to the feelings of people in nature, and none are willing to give up their lives for Christs sake and the Gospels, until they become convinced of the necessity of it, but it appears to me from my own experience and reading, that if there is any reality in religion which I believe there is, that the work in which we are engaged is the work of God, and that it will go on until all come to the knowledge of the truth, when life and death will be set before every individual. Much might be said on this subject, but my head is very weak, and I find that as the warm weather approaches it becomes more so.

Richard McNemar is now with us[38] and expects to remain here a few days and perhaps longer. He spent the
Winter I believe in Indianna and is at this time upon his
return home. He sends his love to you. I can make Samuel[39]
wellcome to my name as long as he is willing to bear it. My
opinion of him, as well as of Jane,[40] is the same that it allways has been, for I allways believed that the disposition
of both of them was very good. Evelyn desired me to tell
you that if you ever intended giving her any thing more
that she would be glad you would send it to her now. She
told me at the same time that she had been so long without
receiving any thing from you, that she had given it over
alltogether and did not expect you for the future to provide
her with any thing.

I again met with Howard Randolph[41] at Chaumiere. He
is a very different man from Patrick, and is I believe as
good as he knows how to be. He has been some time there
and will in all probability settle himself in Kentucky but
cannot like many others receive the doctrines of the Believers.

I remain with great regard,

Your Son,
W S Byrd

PS. Brother Henry [Miller] disires to be remembered to
you and John [Shain] likewise, who says he could give you
a hearty shake by the hand.

[Pleasant Hill, Mid-May, 1827]

[Dear Father,]

The author[42] of the above letter whom you well know desired me to finish his epistle and send it on to you. As he has in contemplation a journey to Union Village in a short time, you will in all probability see him, as he told me that if he should go to the State of Ohio he would call upon you at your residence. You will I expect receive a letter from me in a few days.

Uncle Woodson did not sell his property, but has a part of it under cultivation, and his buildings occupied. The time I write to you will depend upon my feelings, as I know you would wish. Francis and Leonard went off this morning to Frankfort, where the Federal Court is now in session. I allways have the inclination to communicate with you either in person, or on paper, but what I mean and you no doubt comprehend me is that some times I am more capable of conveying my ideas with facility, than at others, for although I am something like the young man you have often told me about, who said while in conversation on the subject, that he was frequently at a loss as well for ideas as words to express them, yet I am favord in this way so much, as occasionally to have a few ideas, with words to express them after a fashion. Remember me if you please to your family.

[W S Byrd]

Pleasant Hill, May 25th, 1827

Dear Father,

I received your favour of the 24th, and feel thankfull to you for the counsel relative to my health contained in it. Attention to our regimin I believe to be all important for the restoration, as well as for the preservation of health, and the longer I live the more am I convinced of the necessity of preserving the equilibrium, between the different parts of the human system, the organick, the animal, and the intellectual. I was pleased with your invitation, and delivered your message to our Sister Asuby. Her health is still delicate, and I have no doubt but that a journey to your residence in pleasant weather would be beneficial to her.

Some changes have taken place in the Society since you left us, and a number have gone away. Among those that have apostatised a few in the young order have married, making good the words of the Apostle when speaking of those that had come to the knowledge of the truth, and received the faith of Christ which was not to marry. All this has not discouraged me, but on the contrary it has rather had a tendency to increase my faith, as it goes to shew that the harvest of the Lord has come, and that his reapers have gone forth. I am not at all surprised at Aunt Page[43] for exclaiming against the Believers. I suppose she would with Aunt Massie,[44] and other professors, scof at the idea of Christs making his second appearance in Ann Lee. How great therefore will be the mortification of these professors, when they come to know that the same Christ that dwelt in Jesus of Nazareth, appeared the second time in this female, the spiritual Mother of all the new creation of God, and that he is now on earth judging the world in his people, the saints of the most high. Christs people are not of this world, and therefore the world know them not, but all good Believers have the satisfaction to know that they are of God, that they are owned by him, and reserved for the enjoyment of that peace and happiness which passeth all understanding, and which hath not entered into the imagination of mankind in an unregenerate state even to conceive.

In your letter to Francis I observe you again mentioned the cross. I have not heard him say any thing particularly on the subject, but do suppose that if we were all together in conversation as I observed to him, after the perusal of your letter, there would be no difference in our ideas on the subject, for although from our letters there appears to be some, I suppose if we understood each other we would be of the same mind, as all good Believers have but one faith, one Lord, and one baptism. I do not know that any thing I may have written on the subject was entitled to any weight, and do therefore almost regret that I wrote any thing about the cross which was calculated to call forth a reply, and expose my ignorance. You did not say whether you intended to visit us alone in the latter part of the summer, or whether you calculated on bringing your family with you. From your not mentioning them, I was rather disposed to believe that they would not accompany you.

Elder Samuel Turner, has been absent for some weeks on a visit to Union Village. He went over in company with Richard McNemar, and the Ministry from South Union, who wished to call at Union Village on their way to New Lebanon. I incline to believe from all that I have heard that Richard McNemar, or Mathew Houston[45] will return with Elder Samuel Turner, and continue here until the Fall.

Leonard did not go to the State of Ohio as I wrote you I expected he would do, but has been admitted into one of the families of the young order of Believers, where I hope he can content himself without any more molesting the

young Sisters in their duty, in order as he wrote you to as-
certain what progress they are making in the work of God.
He did not say so expressly, but this may be collected from
his conversation, and writing. Whatever may have been his
motives, no good Believers could approbate such conduct,
as I told him, but at the same time I believe he was sincere
in what he wrote you on the subject, and that if he was
prompted to act as he did from any other consideration
than what he professed to you, he was blinded by the flesh,
which is as he calls it, a badge of deception. I give this as
my opinion on his conduct, without seting up my judgment in opposition to those who are before me.

A young Lawyer, a native of Connecticut, lately called
here in the stage, and made application for boarding for a
few days. While he was with us, he read the Testimony, and
the Manifesto, apparently with great attention, particularly the former, occasionally conversing with John. After
remaining here near a week, he paid his bill, and directly
afterwards communicated to John with tears, and afterwards to Elder Sister Charity, his determination to forsake
the world, and form a Union with the believers, which he
did, and is now according to his age a promising member
of the Society. This information I supposed would be pleasing to you, and I therefore thought I would communicate
it. I must now conclude this letter and remain

Yours in love,
W S Byrd

William Henry Brown is the Lawyer's name. He appears
to be a man of a liberal education, good talents, and
learned in the law. Remember me to the family.

Pleasant Hill, July 24th, 1827[46]

Dear Father,

As the present is a time of great confusion in the Society I shall not write much, but knowing that you have in contemplation a visit to this place in a very short time, I thought it my duty to address you, if only to inform you of the state of things as they now exist at Pleasant Hill, but at the same time I do assure you, that I never took up my pen to perform a more disagreeable task, but being fully satisfyed that if you were as well acquainted with the situation of the Society as I am, you would postpone your visit.

Before I determined to take this course I consulted Francis, and Elder Eleazar,[47] the latter after conversing with the ministry on the subject, directed me to request you to postpone your visit, one month, to set off from Sinking Spring on the 7th of September instead of the time proposed by yourself. Benjamin S Youngs, and his companions, in the ministry, that accompanied him to the East, is expected here at that time, and will be able to give you information which you would wish to receive, and which could not be obtained before that time.

Yours in love
W S Byrd

Pleasant Hill, July the 31st, 1827

Dear Father,

In my last communication I omitted to request from you a reply as soon as convenient. Upon reflection afterwards I concluded to address you again, and more at length, as I have no reason to believe that letters from Pleasant Hill will be at any time burthensome to you.

Soon after I last wrote to you, Elder Samuel expressed
some apprehension that your mind might be perplexed to
know, what I meant in my letter to you, by confusion in the
Society. I told him that I was satisfied that after the correspondence between us on the subject, you would comprehend my meaning by the expression, and attribute it all to
the true cause, which is apostacy, and it might naturally
be supposed where so many leave a Society as have gone
from here since you left us, there would be some male-
contents, and of course something like confusion. Nevertheless for the satisfaction of Elder Samuel who I suppose
is not quite as well acquainted with his brother Charles, as
I am, I thought it my duty to come to a particular explanation. For myself, I have no idea that you would be atall
shaken in your faith, if half the Society should at one time
forsake the way of life, because I feel confident that you are
upon a foundation which cannot be moved. So far indeed
from our being discouraged by any thing of this kind may
we not rejoice in union with all good believers, in behold-
ing the work of God going on, a work which will make a
final separation between good and evil. But as what I have
said is intended for an explanation, and not for an exhor-
tation, it is time for me to leave this subject, and I will only
add that in my opinion this falling away goes conclusively
to shew, and if my mind had not been satisfied of it before,
it would be fully so now, that there is on Pleasant Hill a
righteous, godly people, with whom the wicked cannot
dwell. You will not I suppose infer from any thing I have
written that our ministry, or any of the believers entertain
doubts of your honesty, or think lightly of your faith, for on
the contrary from all that I have heard from them, I can
without hesitation say, that they are highly pleased with
your faith and honesty, and feel disposed to do any thing in

their power to promote your temporal and eternal well-fare.

Your connection Uncle Samuel Woodson, has gone to witness the reality of an unseen world. He departed this life at Chaumiere, last Saturday morning, after a short, and painfull illness of one week. The disease which terminated his earthly career is called the inflamation in the brain. How uncertain is human existence, it has been but a short time since he was here with his son Tucker, both apparently in the enjoyment of good health. His daughter Sally is at this time lying sick at Frankfort, and will in all probability share the same fate. All this information you will not be surprised to receive after their removal from the healthiest, to the most sickly part of the State.

Evelyn went to Frankfort to supply the place of her Aunt who was sent for from Chaumiere, to attend her husband, or I might perhaps with more propriety say, to be an unprofitable witness of the distressing scene, for I do suppose that there was as little prospect of her being able to administer relief to her husband, as there was of Evelyns rendering any service to her daughter. Is it not strange that Evelyns Grandparents, should suffer her to visit such a place at this season of the year.[48] Had She been in the possession of usefull medical knowledge, and a nurse of the first order, it might be accounted for, but as it is I am at a loss to know what object they could possibly have had in view. Since you wrote to me I have received a letter from her, in which she complains much of your neglectful treatment towards her.

A few months ago I concluded a letter agreeable to Leonards request, which he had commenced and addressed to you, but as you did not acknowledge the receipt of it in your last I suppose it miscarried. He desired me to remember him to you in my next letter, and tell you that although in the opinion of others he was standing still, that he was confident himself he was making rapid progress in the work of regeneration. Brother Rufus left this place last sunday morning, for Union Village in company with Nathaniel Sharp[49] of that place. It is expected that he will go on from there to New Lebanon, and return with the company that went from South Union. Joel Shields, formerly an Elder in the centre house,[50] now lives here in the place of John Shane, who became tired of his situation, and James Guest [Gass] the former companion of our sister Lucy, is the first Elder in the centre house in the place of Joel Shields, who as I have just mentioned above, resides at this place. The ministry join me in love to you, and all the family, and should nothing unexpected occur to prevent it will expect to see you here at the time proposed in my letter, which I suppose you received. The Society in general as far as I can learn are in the enjoyment of their usual good health. All the good believers are anxious to see you here, and no doubt feel much concerned for the necessity which induced them through me, to request you, to postpone your visit. With great regard your son,

W S Byrd

Pleasant Hill, August 20th, 1827

Dear Father,

Your favour of the 7th instant has been received. The perusal of your letter of the 30th ultimo to brother Francis, wherein you give him an account of the continuation of your chronick disease, has created in my mind much concern, as I am disposed from my acquaintance with the constitutions of men of your age, to attribute it to the long use of medicines ignorantly administered to you, the effects of which cannot easily be removed. I indulge the hope however that a favourable change may yet take place notwithstanding your age, especially as there appears to be some prospect of your removing to a more healthy part of the world.

I am pleased to be able to inform you that the course which you have prescribed for me in relation to exercise is the very one that I have been for some time past pursuing, and can say from experience, that the time you recommend is the best part of the day that a person capable of performing no more than myself, can devote to manuel employ ment.

Your accounts from time to time, of our friend Isaac White[51] and others are pleasing to me. I have a very favourable opinion of him, and believe with you that he is an honest professor of religion, but at the same time feel as little hesitation in saying that he is not a possessor, or in other words that he has not received the Gospel, which is the power of God unto salvation, and of course not a christian. We are not to judge of any people by what they profess, or what they believe, but as you very correctly observed, we are to know them by their fruits, and therefore we may say without fear of present or future condemnation, that all these protestants, however high a profession of religion they may make, are the children of this world still, and not the followers of our Saviour Jesus Christ, who led a life of daily selfdenial and abstainance from every thing that defileth.

Should you come over in a carriage as you expected

when you wrote to brother Francis, I will thank you to bring with you a number of my letters which I think you will find in the press, wrapped up in a large sheet of paper. Two of those letters are directed to you from Dr. Williamson, all that remain if any, are directed to me. Among them you will probably find a copy of Kidders letter.[52] The original is in your possession I suppose, where I wish it to continue, as it may be a satisfaction to you particularly now that you are a member of this Society, to have some thing to remind you of the state of your sons mind just before he passed from time into eternity. I have no desire to read any of these letters at this time, but thought I would like to have them among my other papers.

Brother George[53] has expressed to me in a feeling manner his concern at our not mentioning Powel in our letters, and said that he had thoughts of addressing a letter to him, but was backward about it not knowing how it would be received. I told him that I thought it very doubtfull whether he would get an answer if he was to write, and that I would {hope}fully speak of him in my letters to you if I had any thing to say about him, but as I never received a letter, or even a message from him in my life I should be very much at a loss for something to write about. George likes to hear something about all the family, and I do suppose you would be forward at all times to communicate to him, or any of the Believers any thing concerning your family that would be at all interesting to them.

Since the above was written yours of the 15th instant was handed to me by one of our bretheren. Your account[54] of the two Shakers you met with in Chillecothe and Columbus, as well as the Girl in your place, has excited some interest, and the manner in which you made mention of the two former no small degree of curiosity. I am however very

willing to wait until your arrival here for further information.

I must now I believe conclude this letter, and remain
with great regard

Your Son,
William S Byrd

Pleasant Hill, October 30th, 1827

My Dear Father,

Enclosed I send you a copy of my address to Dr. Williamson.[55] On the same paper you will find the piece written by
Richard McNemar, which you requested me to send you. I
wish you to write to me as soon as you can and give me
some account of your visit to Chaumiere, the state of your
health upon your return home, and of any thing else you
may wish to write about. I do not wish you to give publicity to the within, as I suppose it will soon appear in the
public prints of this State {and} probably circulate elsewhere.[56]

Remember me to your family, including your two young-
est children. The circumstance of your having in your will
made such a difference in their favour, does not in the least
degree lessen my friendly feelings towards them, and an
anxious wish for the temporal and eternal welfare of themselves and their parents. Our bretheren and sisters are in
good health generally, and would if they knew I was writing to you send their united messages of love and friendship, not because you are a new member as Ephram Mc-
Bride[57] professes to believe, but because they consider you
to be an honest soul willing to sacrifice all for Christs sake
and the Gospels. Our Sister Asuby has moved into a room

that has a fire place in it, and I now indulge the hope that she will enjoy a better state of health than she has for some years past.

With great regard

Your Son,
W S Byrd

Pleasant Hill, November the 11th, 1827

My Dear Father,

Agreeable to your request I now take up my pen to inform you that your letter to brother Francis arrived here last evening, and is at this time with its contents, in the safekeeping of brother Edmund.[58] This last has within a few days past moved from this place, to the center house, where he is the principal Elder in place of James Guest, who was tired of that situation. Eldress Betey McCarver,[59] likewise has moved from her place of residence to fill the place of Elder Sister Caroline[60] lately deceased.

If you are sincere in your profession as I believe you to be, you will be able to account, and that in a short time too, for my desire to obtain property to convey away to others. I am now in a situation to make a better use of property far, than I ever was before, and therefore you ought not to be surprised at my desire to possess it. As for a support, the Believers would take care of me if I had no estate atall, real or personal, and therefore it is, together with the love I have for them, I am the more anxious to acquire property. I do not wish you to consider this as persevering on the subject, but to assign a reason for my wish

to own property. If it was in your power to put me in possession of a large estate, it would not promote my individual interest one cent, therefore I am not influenced by selfish motives.

As the following Subject is a very disagreeable one I will
get through it as soon as possible. One of our bretheren
called to me the other day and delivered to me a message
from Molly, sent by a stranger from a tavern in Louisville.
It was as you may suppose that you or myself would go
after her. I suppose you may have heard from her before
this time, but not knowing certainly I thought it my duty
to write, although it may be altogether out of your power,
as it is out of mine, to render her any service.

Since the above was written I received a letter from
Molly requesting me to go after her and to bring her here.
Now was I not well acquainted with her, and disposed to
do so I would no doubt be encouraged by the Believers. But
how could I endure the thought of having her in this Society upon the Believers, in her situation, and more especially as we know from experience almost, that Patrick
could persuade her off again in a few months, and keep her
like a prostitute, until she would again become pregnant.
Altho I cannot comply with her request, she may possibly
be sent here and if she is, my situation will be awfull indeed, for the very thought of it has already had a bad effect
upon me. I feel for her, as I would for any human being in
her situation, but it would seem from the past that nothing
can be done for her. She writes me that they were living in
Indiana, at a place I think called Burlington,[61] where they
were doing well, she herself satisfyed, that Patrick thought
he could make more money at Louisville, and persuaded
her contrary to her inclination, to go there. After their removal he found he could make nothing, and endeavoured

for some time to persuade her to return with him to Jessamine. Upon her final refusal, told her he was out of money
and went off.

    With great regard,

Your Son,
W S Byrd

Pleasant Hill, March the 9th, 1828

Dear Father,

    Your favour of the 11th ultimo was received. I was con-
cerned to hear of the death of our old acquaintance and
servant Lavinia, but the intelligence did not as you may
suppose fill me with that unspeakable horror and distress
which it would have done a few years ago, before I received
the faith of Christs second appearing, but was altogether
in the dark on the subject of religion, of heaven, hell, and
eternity, and did not know although I never believed it
from my heart, but that at death the fate of every individual was unalterably fixed, that as a soul was when it left
the body so it would continue to be forever, without any
possibility of a change. How thankfull then ought we to be
to our God for the Gospel which we have received from
him, through his ever blessed servants Christ and Mother,
for that light and knowledge which will ultimately effec-
tually dispel every doubt, and fear, and leave the soul in
the enjoyment of perfect happiness.

    I received a letter some time ago from Dr. Williamson
which I answered. I should be glad if you could see all that
has passed between him and myself since I have been with
the Believers, especially as a part of it was the composition
of Elder Eleazar[62] which I sent to him in his own name. All

of his letters to me together with my answers to them have been read to the ministry and some others, and I am pleased to be able to inform you that they gave entire satisfaction.

David Spinning,[63] whom we call Elder David, arrived here last evening, and soon after him Elder Eleazar from Union Village, where he has been for some time past. Mother Lucy is still at that place and it is uncertain whether she will ever return here on account of the great opposition that was made to her before she left us. This information may astonish you at first as it did me, but when you consider what a powerfull testimony she bore against sin, and all manner of wickedness, while among us, and the purity of her life and conversation, you will not be at all surprised at the enmity that has been manifested against her by that spirit of evil which is directly opposed to God, and all that is good, and which is still visible in the Society striving for the mastery with unceasing endeavours. But I think we have no cause to fear the consequences of its venome, knowing as we do that the same God that commenced this work, is stronger than the adversary, and will carry it on until the church is thoroughly purged of all evil, and every thing that is contrary to the nature of God and a life of holiness, be done away forever.

As I wrote you my health is better than it was when you were here, and I enjoy more tranquility of mind than I did then, but at the same time I feel it my duty as you are my parent, and one that has expressed a desire to know my situation from time to time, to tell you that although I can write and talk some about happiness, I am far from the enjoyment of that state of felicity which is in reserve for the righteous. On the contrary the life I lead is a life of great, and daily suffering, and this suffering is not a little increased by the view I have of futurity, nevertheless I must confess that I am thankfull for this light that I have been favoured with, and believe from my heart that it is necessary, and that it has been sent to me by an all wise God to enable me the better to bear the cross which he has laid upon me, for although I can sensibly feel the love of God in my soul, and consequently enjoy some happiness, yet it is mixed up with so much mental and bodily affliction, especially the former, that I could not it appears to me keep soul and body together, if it was not for the prospect I have of attaining to that happiness without the least mixture of alloy which God has promised to those who by a patient continuance in welldoing will finally overcome all things.

James Congleton, our elder brother, desired me present his love to you and tell you that he will expect you here again in the ensuing season. The ministry likewise join me in love to you and your family. With great regard,

Your Son,
William S Byrd

Francis has gone to new Harmony[64] to negotiate a sale of the West Union land &c and will I suppose be absent for some weeks.

PS   I have been directed to add that it is the age and infirmity of Mother Lucy that renders her return to this place uncertain, as the same testimony is preached by others and the same holy life led to the great confusion of the enemies of the cross of Christ and to the glory and honour of God and his people.

Your account of your Son Samuels ideas of the relationship existing between him and Mother Ann was truly diverting, and well calculated to excite a smile as it did from some of the Sisters to whom I mentioned it. Samuel as a natural man who as the Apostle tells us cannot discern the things of the Spirit readily concludes according to the rules of consanguinity, that if Mother Ann is your immediate parent she must of course be his grand Mother.

Pleasant Hill, April 13th, 1828

Dear Father,

Your letter of the 22d ultimo was received.[65] I was truly sorry to hear that your health was growing worse instead of better, but at the same time I must confess to you that I was not at all surprised at it, knowing as I do from my own experience, that the practise you have been in for years past of eating only twice a day, instead of the common number of times, is highly pernicious to the health of the constitution, and will if persevered in entirely destroy it. I feel thankfull to you for your advice in relation to diet &c. and believe it to be very good, and hope that you will in turn hearken to mine, and profit by it. Now I believe that it is absolutely necessary for the health of the body, that the stomach should allways be supplied with wholesome food, for the liquid substance that digests our diet which the Drs. you know call the gastrick fluid, is like the human mind which is allways at work upon some thing or other, and if it is not supplied with fresh food once in every six hours through the day, it must become weak, and consequently unable to perform its functions. You are ready to reply perhaps that you have been in the habit of eating twice in the course of the day, for years that use has with you become a second nature, and that therefore you cannot depart from it. This kind of reasoning however, I am qualified from my own knowledge of health, and personal experience, unhesitatingly to pronounce to be erroneous, and that the above mentioned practise is more injurious if any thing than the diet you speak of, and will as certainly destroy the health. Superfluities in living as Tea, Coffee, &c. may become necessaries by long indulgence but these are innocent if temperance is observed in the use of them, and will not even at first, be attended with any serious consequences, not so with unnatural abstainance from food which will cause the stomach to grow weaker and weaker until it is unable to digest food of the most simple quality. This I know from experience, and there fore request that you will adopt the mode of living above prescribed as I am confident you will derive great benefit from it.

I spoke to Elder Eleazar about your observations in relation to miracles, and will probably shew him your letter or that part of it concerning them that I may send you his reflections on the subject as you requested. In the meantime I will give you my opinion in regard to miracles which will I have no doubt correspond with his, for I have found from conversing with him and others about his own age at different times that I have the same ideas on subjects of importance that they have, and I do assure you that it is a source of very great satisfaction to me to reflect upon it and to know that as I grow in age my light and knowledge in the Gospel increases. I will likewise give you my opinion about the punishment of the wicked for I feel no unwillingness to answer any question according to my ability that you may think proper to put to me.

As for miracles I believe that the power of performing them exists as much in this Church, as in any of the eastern Churches, though not as often exercised, inasmuch as I believe that the same Allmighty that reigns in them, dwels in this also. I moreover believe with you that the present is a day for wonderfull works as well as for good works, that they go together, and that wherever there is a church of Christ they will be performed. It was my intention when I commenced writing to have said much more on this subject, but I believe I will not prosecute it any further as I expect you will receive some communication from Elder Eleazar and in that way know my opinion fully. After all the conversations I have had with you from time to time I must confess that I was not a little surprised at the question you put to me about the wicked, and still more so when you advanced your opinion. I was surprised because it is a topick that of all others seemed to occupy the least place in your thoughts when I was with you, and one on which you allways manifested an unwillingness to converse {with me}.

You say that you do not believe in the salvation of all persons, and at the same time reject the doctrine of an endless punishment. Now if this is your opinion just as you have expressed it I am at a loss to know what is to become of a fellow that is neither eternally saved nor damned, for we are taught to believe that the Gospel will be preached to all, and that it will prove a savour of life unto life, or of death unto death, to them that hear it. If I understand the meaning of your words they surely do not convey the ideas you intended to communicate. For myself, I believe that salvation is offered to all persons without exception and that it is in the power of every individual alike to obtain it, for it is not the will of God that any should perish but that all should come in and be saved. But at the same time he has created man a free agent with knowledge to discern between good and evil and if he will contrary to his better judgment reject the Gospel on account of the cross it brings with it to his carnal corrupt nature, he will most assuredly incur the divine displeasure with all its awfull consequences. I am pleased with your invitation for me to visit you and spend at least half my time with you. I can form a very correct idea of your feelings situated as you are in the world, surrounded by the people of it, without any connexion with them, and can from my heart sympathise with you. I was much diverted with the account you gave of Powel, and cannot help thinking that if we could allways find some thing of that kind to laugh at in unpleasant subjects it would as you suppose have a great tendency to banish uncomfortable feelings. I do not myself live altogether in the way that I have recommended to you above but at the same time I know it to be the most healthy way of living, and therefore advise you to adopt it.

With great regard

Your Son,
William S Byrd

Pleasant Hill, 18th of May, 1828

Dear Father,

Your favour of the 22d ultimo was received. Soon after its arrival, I endeavoured to answer it, but after writing a few lines found my mind in such a week state in consequence of bodily indisposition, that I determined to postpone it until I should recover my usual health, and now allthough it is not as good as common I can write with something like comfort, and feel it my duty to address you if only to let you know that I am getting better and not past writing.

I was pleased to hear you say that you could unite with me in allmost all my opinions on different subjects excepting one on which you said your mind was not fully satisfyed, but at the same time advanced an opinion which you said might possibly change. I feel no hesitation in telling you that your ideas on that subject will be very different some time hence, because I am confident in my own mind that such an opinion is not only unscriptural, but contrary to reason, and all the attributes of God, who when he created man breathed into his nostrils as we are told the breath of life whereby he became a living soul. Now I believe that this breath or Spirit that God breathed into Adam, when he created him, is in every individual, that it is as immortal as the source from whence it came, and must exist forever. By taking detached parts of Scripture allmost any doctrine may be established, but if you form your opinions from the whole of it as I know you are generally inclined to do, it appears to me that you would come to a much more consistent conclusion about the future state of the wicked. You will not I hope consider what I have said as a reflection upon you, but merely an attempt to divest you of an opinion which I consider to be erroneous, for I know that there is something in the mind of man that revolts at the idea of an endless punishment.

For myself, I believe that Gods object in creating man was to make him honourable, and happy, and thereby promote his own glory, and that although he became lost from him by disobedience that he has provided a way whereby all souls may be saved that will come down and submit to it. But the way of God is so contrary to the feelings of mankind in a state of nature, that they will prefer their sensual enjoyments until they receive so much light and knowledge of the necessity of bearing a cross against them, that they can take no pleasure in them. Now this must be the case with all sooner or later, and whether every individual will be wise and accept the salvation of God on his own terms when offered to them, is a question that no mortal can determine, but at the same time we may exercise our reason, and form opinions from Scripture, and the attributes of God, and be as well established in them allmost as if an Angel of God was to come down from heaven and tell us that it was so according as we believed. But if I know beyond a doubt that all souls would finally be saved, I should feel an unwillingness to communicate such light to others, not that I should be affraid of rendering you or any Believer with good faith and understanding atall careless on the subject, because I do not believe that it would make any difference with you, that it would not in the least degree check your progress in the work of redemption, knowing as you do that it is only as the flesh dies, that the spirit rises into life. But such a faith would have a very different effect upon a common worldling without the knowledge of the way of salvation, it would render him easy and comfortable in the flesh, and place him farther from the light of the Gospel than he was before, when perhaps he had doubts and fears upon the subject.

I was pleased to hear that the experiment which you made upon your health was attended with success for a time, and hope that you will be able to continue it.

If Powel could be satisfyed to engage in some {fine} business, and apply himself to it regularly without going so far as to injure his health, I think he would become more cheerfull in his mind, and less disposed to quarrel with the family. He is still young and will find it much easier to change his manner of life now, than in a few years hence, when perhaps he will be visited by the complaints which commonly afflict the sedentary as they advance in years. Your summer session comes on if I am not mistaken in the month of July and I fear that you will have a very uncomfortable time if you attend. I should be much pleased if some of your influential friends in Congress[66] would exert themselves to get an alteration in the terms of your court so as to enable you to stay at home during the inclement seasons of the year as I have no doubt but that your health is allways injured by it. Our Elder Sister[67] has been confined for some time past in consequence of a hard fall, but I hope she will recover soon, as I understand the hurt though very painfull, was not dangerous. The rest of the Society I think are generally well, with the exception of a few labouring under chronick diseases. The Ministry join me in love to you, and likewise our sister Azubah, who expressed in a most feeling manner her ardent wish for the prosperity and happiness of yourself and family. I must now conclude this letter with the wish that you may recover a better state of health, and remain with great regard,

Your Son,
William S Byrd

Pleasant Hill, 19th of June, 1828

Dear Father,

I received your last letter containing some powders, for which I wish you to receive my thanks as well as for your lengthy communication on the subject of health. I would have acknowledged the receipt of it sooner, had I not just written to you informing you of the improvement in my health. During my sickness which was not atall dangerous, though very disagreeable, I was attended by one of our bretheren, a son of Elisha Thomas,[68] a Physician, who administered to me salutary medicines, and among the rest, those very powders you recommended mixed up with some other medicine. I have not the least apprehension of an early dissolution from bodily indisposition, but at the same time I feel much anxiety on the subject of health as I am occasionally in a very uncomfortable situation by reason of my infirmity.

The Society continues to decrease in number, though I hope not in quality, for on the contrary I do confidently believe that there is an increase in the body, of righteousness and peace, but to mention the names of those who do from time to time apostatise would be tedious to me, and perhaps uninteresting to yourself, as you know but few of them. I therefore have generally omitted to record in my letters the names of those that leave us, I will now however mention two members a man and his wife with whom you were acquainted, and you will I have no doubt be surprised to receive the intelligence if you have not heard it already, as they were both at the time you were with us for any thing you knew to the contrary, prominent Believers— namely Elder James Guest, and Lucy his wife. Lucy continued here some months after her husband went away, during which time he visited her occasionally, and she poor creature whom you once considered allmost a saint on earth, like her Mother Eve, listened to the arguments of the enemy of souls until she was finally overcome. As I mentioned above I expect you will be surprised to hear of the fall of Lucy and her husband, but at the same time if you were as well acquainted with them, and their history as I am, you would not be in the least affected by it.

We hear occasionally from Mother [Lucy Smith], she has noticed me several times since she left us in a very particular manner, with kind messages of love and friendship, which is as you may suppose highly pleasing to one, who has forsaken the world, and all natural connexions, in order to gain a union and relationship with the righteous, an inheritance which fadeth not away. Elder Benjamin left here this morning after a visit of some weeks which I hope will be attended with happy results, as he acquitted himself well during his stay here in his holy function. He desired me to give his love to you, with a fervent wish for your prosperity and happiness.

After the above was written your letter to brother Francis was handed to me. From the perusal of it I am induced to apprehend that my last to you miscarried. It was put in the office the same day and by the same person that took yours containing the powders out of it. I must now I believe conclude and remain Your Son,

With true regard,
William S Byrd

P S   After sealing up my letter I was not able to send it on as soon as I expected, and feeling a desire notwithstanding the miscarriage of my last, to fill up the sheet, I determined to open it and add something more, as you have expressed your satisfaction with my lengthy communications. In one of your former letters you gave me an account of your great forbearance with Powel, when contending with your companion, and expressed an opinion that if you were not a member of this Church you would be unable to remain in silence, but would have to interpose in favour of the latter. Now for myself, I believe that if you are united in spirit to the body of Christ, you are in possession of that power of God which you never had before, and which will enable you to bear and suffer all things. But at the same time I have no idea that a mere profession of this religion, and a formal union with the Believers, will give you any more power over evil than you had previous to your joining this society, and I incline to think that you will unite with me in this opinion. Therefore my only object in speaking of it is to induce you in future to be more particular in the expression of your sentiments. In the same letter you returned your thanks to our ever blessed Mother for this power, as you did likewise in former letters for other blessings. Now I believe I have as much respect and love for the female part of the Deity as you have, but at the same time I know that we have a heavenly Father, as well as a heavenly Mother, and it appears to me that his name ought allways to be mentioned when returning thanks in union with hers. This you used to do, but not hearing any thing of it lately I did not know but that you had forgotten the nature of our heavenly parentage.

Pleasant Hill, July 14th, 1828

Dear Father,

I suppose from your late letter to Francis that you will be absent at the time this letter reaches your place, but still I thought I ought to write in order that you may find an answer to your last of the 8th to me upon your return home. As soon as I received your letter I handed it over to Francis for his perusal. After reading it he expressed his surprise at the inference you drew from an expression he happened to drop when writing to you on the subject of your funds.[69] He requested me to tell you that half of the property mortgaged, was more than sufficient to pay the debt, and that the Society would at any time most cheerfully take it, and advance the amount. I do not think you have any reason to be concerned on the subject, but on the contrary confidently believe that you did well in placing your money in the hands of brother Francis, and that you will have no cause to repent it.

As for the rent accruing from the tract of land to which you made an allusion in your letter I do not know that you would be much the richer at the end of the year for the receipt of it, and if I am not very much mistaken you told me in the last conversation we had on the subject that you would say nothing about rent, and I do not think you ought to demand it, at any rate while the farm remains undivided and in the care of a Society whose agent has done so much to promote your pecuniary interest. You are free however to act as you please on this occasion as you know, but at the same time I thought I would remind you of the conversation that past between us, and hope you will excuse the liberty I have taken with you. I feel disposed to write more on this subject, but as you were not pleased with the purchase of the farm at first, and afterwards made the last payment merely to release the Society, I will proceede no farther but leave you to act on this occasion according to the dictates of your own conscience.

In your letter you mention our friend Burgess. It has been so long since you wrote any thing about him that I had begun to think there was no communication of any kind between you at this time. I was pleased to hear of him and have no doubt but that his receipt for the teeth may be beneficial to the generality of people as I have allways viewed him as a man of good judgment, with a usefull stock of medical knowledge. I wrote to him some time after I came here, and as I never got an answer I incline to think my letter miscarried. I will thank you to ask him about it the next time you see him for I took some pains with it, and it would be a satisfaction to me to hear that it was received. I believe I will now conclude as I do not suppose you have yet seen my letter of last week, and remain with true regard your Son,

W S Byrd[70]

APPENDIXES

A

Questions to Believers by Charles Willing Byrd and Answers from the Shakers[1]

In coming a journey of two days[2] to see you and to make enquiries, I am not actuated by an idle curiosity, but by a desire to obtain useful information on a subject of vital importance. I therefore request you to bear and forbear with me.

Perhaps you would wish that I should give some account of myself, before I proceed to ask any questions.

Other denominations of Christians believe that they are in the road of salvation. Do you *know* that you are; and if you do, how do you know it?

In this day of full redemption,[3] as you consider it, do you suppose yourselves to be more spiritual than Paul was?

If the work of redemption, which is a substance, is alone to be given to the world, and no sign is to be given them, how can they distinguish between your sincerity and that of the Methodists, w[h]o profess all that you profess, excepting what relates to the matrimonial tie?

When our Saviour said "before the flood they did marry, eat and drink,"[4] why did he couple marriage with eating and drinking?

What did the Apostle mean, when he said, "if any man think that he behaveth himself uncomely towards his virgin, if she pass the flour of her age and need so require, let him do what he will, he sinneth not, let them marry"?[5]

When the same Apostle says, "what I would, that I do not, but what I hate, that I do"; and when he says, "if I do that I would not, it is no more I that do it, but sin that dwelleth in me";[6] is it not an admission that even after he was Christs, sin remained in him unconquered?

And when he says "I have fought the good fight, I have finished my course, I have kept the faith":[7] does he not mean that *faith* was the good fight, as nothing here is said about works?

Again when he says, "henceforth there is laid up for me a crown of righteousness"[8] &c; does he not look forward to a future state for the resurrection, or redemption from sin?

101

If by the present work of God, Believers grow up into the Divine nature *by degrees* resisting and overcoming fleshy lusts &c; what does the Apostle of the Gentiles mean by saying, "we shall not all sleep, but we shall all be changed in the twinkling of an eye, at the last trump"?[9]

How long is it before the resurrection takes place in most believers among you?

Do you consider true believers to be subject to dull and lively frames of mind, sometimes confident, sometimes doubting their salvation?

How soon does inward depravity leave you, I mean the greater number of you?

Have you other books communicating information to the world respecting your community, besides "Christs Second appearing"?[10]

Have you any other rules except those contained in that volume?

Have you among yourselves any other signs and wonders still, besides the work of redemption?

Do you refrain from work on the Sabbath, and if you do, is it for conscience sake, or from respect towards your neighbours?

Do you pray, and if you do, do you pray aloud?

Have you still the gift of discerning spirits?

Have you still the gift of healing; and if you have, do you exercise it only for the benefit of yourselves, and can you by means of it cure complaints of long standing?

Has there been any recent change in the opening of the testimony?

Are backsliders common among you?

In what are children educated among you?

Are Doctors ever called in, or have you any Physicians in your community?

How do you reconcile the circumstances of Davids being a favourite of God's with his having so many wives and concubines?

Is death bed sickness among you at all different from {what it} is among other professors?

How often do you worship?

In labouring, are no persons ever censured in any way for the little they perform, and do they never at any time receive any mark of disapprobation?

What is the amount of your population in the Village,[11] and what the whole number of Believers in the United States?

If you sell the proceeds of your manual labour, would a new member differently situated, be permitted to sell the proceeds of his intellectual labour, and yet be viewed as one having a claim to full membership?

Do any of you ever walk or ride merely for the benefit of your health?

How is your community situated with respect to longevity?

Are ministers sent out to preach to the world?

[Answers][12]

In answer to the enquiries on the preceeding pages, the Believers informed me in substance, that they had the witness within themselves of their being in the resurrection, an experimental conviction in their bosoms of the absence of the works of the flesh, pointed out in Gal. v. 19. 20. 21. and in feeling and enjoying the fruit of the Spirit, discribed in the same epistle and in the same chapter, verses 22. 23.

That they believe they have the advantages which Paul had, with additional light.

That the world can only judge of their being and acting up to their profession, by an attention and impartial observation of their conduct, and from the consideration of their having lived together in harmony among themselves since their regular establishment, which has been for twenty eight years, without a law suit and without a reference to a church meeting for a settlement of differences or any thing of the kind.

That when eating and drinking are mentioned in the Bible, it is a reference to feasting.

That Paul in addressing the carnal Corinthians had to feed them with milk instead of strong food, and if they were really ignorant of the act of uncleaness between the sexes, even between man and wife, being sinful, and they acted honestly according to the light they had, they were not guilty of a sin in marrying under certain circumstances.

That when the Apostle says if "I do that I would not, It is no more I that do it, but sin that dwelleth in me,"[13] an attentive notice of the manner of pointing the different sentences will shew, that he was discribing what he had been, when he was himself unconverted, and also the situation of the carnal man who had some correct ideas and feelings.

That a view of the whole Scriptures will shew, that faith without works, is no faith atall.

That Paul certainly looked forward to this day of resurrection, when he says "we shall not all sleep, but we shall all be changed."[14]

That true Believers are not subject to dull and lively frames of mind; sometimes confident and sometimes doubting; but that when they get into bed at night, they are "indeffereant in their choice, to sleep or die."

That the change which takes place in them is gradual, until the way, by becoming more and more straight, one step shewing the way to another, leads to the resurrection even in this life.

That they have no rules or covenant among them, unless what is contained in the book entitled "The Testimony of Christs Second appearing," is so denominated.

That at present there are among them no other Signs and wonders, than the fruit of the Spirit; nor the gifts of healing, miracles, and so on.

That they practise silent prayer, and adopt the worship of dancing agreeably to the Scriptures.

That Backsliders are as common among them as among the different sects.

That Doctors attend the sick, and that they have Physicians of their own community.

That persons on their death bed among them, evince more equanimity than other people manifest under similar circumstances.

That a reference to dates will shew, that when David was a "man after God's own heart,"[15] he was not at that time an adulterous and a murderer.

That no one is censured in the Society for not labouring more than he chooses to do.

That some of them continually walk and ride merely for health.

That their Society is situated like others with respect to longevity.

That the members are permitted if they like it, to sell the proceeds of their manual or intellectual labour, but that from *inclination* they will soon decline it.

That their population in Union Village, is six hundred, near two thousand in the Western States, and alltogether about four thousand; all of whom as far as they know and believe are in the United States. That the Sabbath is their only day of general worship, but that each family (their families consist of from forty to sixty persons) will worship every night and morning.

Sinking Spring   *C W Byrd*
Oct 25th 1825

P.S. In answer to other and farther inquiries, they said that the Hebrew sentence, which was construed as saying, "Be angry and sin not; let not, the sun go down upon thy wrath,"[16] was not according to the correct translation, which says, "do not sin by getting angry, but if you should be overtaken by it, do not continue in it." That there is a perfect equality in the living of each and of all of their members in diet, clothing, and every thing else.

In answer to the suggestion that their own writers admitted the frailty of Ann Lee, by acknowledging that she was the mother of several children, before she discovered that Christ was in her: whereas the Apostles who were the biographers of our Saviour Jesus Christ, drew him as a perfect character; they said that it was unimportant at what period of her life she was anointed, whether at twelve years old, or earlier, or at the middle age; that it was not[17]

B

A Business Proposition from
Francis Voris to Charles Willing Byrd[18]

Pleasant Hill, September 16th, 1826

I will Submit the following to brother Charles by way of Proposition for his consideration.

We will take the one half of the McMurtry[19] tract and pay to Taylor[20] in two annul instalments five hundred and fifteen dollars each, making together One thousand and thirty dollars, which is the half of the price of the purchace made of McMurtry.

The division of this tract to be equal between us and your Son in number of Acres, if so can be, to be of equal value and rightly dividing the improvements, and if not to be according to quantity and quality. You and William (if his health will permit) will go with me if you Choose to make the division some day next week, or at any future period you may fix upon. You will then take the title to the whole of Taylors tract—William to the half or one hundred and twenty four acres of the McMurtry tract and we will take title to the residue.

We make this Proposition, Solely to the end that it may be convenient for you to procure Taylors tract. There is quite a Solicitude felt by a good many of the members that you would make this purchase; and they would be willing to do any reasonable thing or duty in order that it might be within your Convenience to do so.

If it should be quite convenient for yourself I will like to hear your Conclusion by Monday in order the better to know how to opperate with Taylor.[21]

In love
Francis Voris

C

The Deed to the Byrd Farm in Kentucky[22]

This Indenture made the [21st] day of October in the year 1826 between William McMurtry & Priscilla his wife of Mercer County and State of Kentucky of the One Part and Charles Willing Byrd of Highland County & State of Ohio & William Silone Byrd of Mercer County and State of Kentucky of the Other Part Witnesseth That the Said William and Priscilla his wife for and in Consideration of the Sum of Two thousand and Sixty Dollars lawful money of the United States to them in hand paid by the Said Charles & William the receipt whereof they do hereby acknowledge have granted bargained and Sold aliend enfeoffed and Confirmed and by there Presents doth grant bargain and Sell Alien enfeoff and confirm unto the Said Charles Willing and William Silone Byrd their Heirs & Assigns forever One Certain Tract or Parcel of land containing Two hundred and forty eight Acres it being apart of a tract Patented to Robertson[23] & McMurtry Situate lying and being in Mercer County on Cedar run and is the tract on which the Said William & Priscilla now lives and bounded as follows, to wit, Beginning at a Hickory, Ash and hackberry Corner to Epperson[24] on the Original line of Robertson & McMurtry and running from thence N 86½ E 156 Poles to a Stake at the end of a line Another Corner to Epperson thence Si E 90 po to a rock in Coghills branch;[25] thence N 88 E 133 po to a flat rock near the mouth of Coghills branch in the original Patent line thence N 27 W. 56 po to a mulberry on the Bank of Cedar run; thence N. 43. E 34 poles to a Stone in Open ground on the Original patent line; thence N 2 W 34 poles to two dogwoods in Said line; thence W 50 po.s to two Beeches Corner to the Shakers thence N 9 W 60 po thence N. 30 W 30 po thence N 20 W 27 poles to a Stone in the Shakers line; thence S 74¾ W 132 poles to two Sugar trees; thence S 10 E 22 poles to a hickory Elm and hackberry; thence N 82½ W 24 poles to two Blue ashes thence S. 10. E 23 poles to a Stake by a drain thence S. 69 W 50 poles to a black walnut on the Original Patent line thence S 70 poles to the Beginning with its appurtenances to have and to hold the Said tract or

Parcel of land with its appurtenances unto the Said Charles W & William S. Byrd and their Heirs and Assigns forever to their only Proper use and behoof and the Said William McMurtry and Priscilla his wife for themselves their Heirs Exttors and Admitted Said tract or Parcel of land with its appurtenances unto the Said Charles and William and their Heirs and Assigns forever against the Claim or Claims of them the Said William and Priscilla their Heirs Exttors and Adm.s and against the Claim or Claims of all and every Other Person or Persons will warrant and forever desired.

In Testimony wheof the Said William McMurtry & Priscilla his wife have hereunto Subscribed their names and affixed their Seals the day and year first within written.

Wm. McMurtry {Seal}

Priscilla her X mark McMurtry {Seal}

Mercer County Ky. Oct. 21st. 1826[26]

The foregoing Indenture was this day Produced to me in my Office and acknowledged by William McMurtry and Priscilla his wife aparty thereto to be their Act and Deed and the Said Priscilla being examined by me Seperate and apart from her Said Husband freely and Voluntarely relinquished her right of Dower to the within mentioned land as the law directs whereupon I have made the Same of record.

Att Tho Allen Ck

A Letter from William S. Byrd
to Doctor Williamson[27]

Pleasant Hill, October 28th, 1827

Friend Williamson,

Upon the receipt of your last letter I thought I would postpone writing for a time as I supposed you would receive with prejudice any thing that I might communicate on the subject of salvation and the cross. Upon further reflection however I determined to write, and now return the questions you propounded to me, and in my opinion fairly and fully answered agreeable to your request by one of our bretheren from Ohio Richard McNemar.

I would have answered them myself, but recollecting your declaration that you wanted to Judge of this Society by their own professions, I thought it would be more satisfactory to you to receive from the pen of an older member some account of our faith. For myself I have no confidence in professions unless they are accompanied with correspondent good works for the tree is to be known by its fruit, and I do therefore know and am not deceived that the faith of the Believers in Christs Second Appearing is the faith of the son of God, because their works are good, and an evil tree cannot bring forth good fruit.

I will now conclude lest there may not be room on this sheet for the following questions and answers. With great regard I remain your friend,

William S Byrd

Question. Do you believe the scriptures of the old and new Testaments to be the inspired Word of God! And do you believe that these scriptures contain all the knowledge that is necessary to our salvation thro faith in Christ Jesus? See 2d Tim *iiid* 15. 16.

To answer this question understandingly is it necessary to define what is meant by "*the inspired word of God.*" Such a form of expression is not to be found in the scriptures. The word inspire or inspiration signifies *a drawing in of the breath, or the infusion of ideas into the mind by a supernatural or divine influence.* The inspiration of God is the receiving of the breath or spirit of God, men are capable of receiving the divine breath or spirit, they are the proper subjects of inspiration; things inanimate are not. Moses was an inspired man, the prophets were inspired. The spirit of inspiration rested on Christ. The Apostles also were inspired, and many since their day have had a measure of divine inspiration. What was spoken by those inspired persons was called the word of God part of which was recorded. This we call a record of the word of God in past ages, and according to the above cited scripture is profitable to furnish the man of God with suitable matter for his work, but it is still the man of God that possesses the spirit and not the book; the spirit of God is not in the book but in the man; it is therefore the person whether man or woman, that contains all the knowledge necessary to salvation. The person and not the book is the proper subject of faith in Christ Jesus, and is capable of ministering the same faith to others. Timothy from a child knew the old Testament, but faith in Christ Jesus was necessary to his salvation. Ye search the scriptures (said Christ) for in them ye think ye have eternal life (but they were mistaken) and they are they that testify of me and ye will not come to me that ye might have life."[28] "Him whom God hath sent ye receive not"[29] etc. The Eunuch had the scriptures but they could not minister to him either the faith or knowledge necessary to salvation. "Understandest thou what thou readest" (said Philip). His answer is a reproof to the protestant world. "How can I except some man guide me."[30]

Question. Do you believe that God has given to man any other revelation of himself and the way of salvation besides what is contained in the book commonly called the bible, if so where is this revelation to be found and by what miracles was it authenticated?

Answer. This question must be impertinent, if the self evident truth is admitted that man and not inanimate matter is the proper subject of inspired knowledge. What knowledge of God or of salvation is contained in the most gilted book more than any other idol framed by human art? To imagine that knowledge, faith or any other intellectual gift is communicable to or from the letters of a book is a gross perversion of the scriptures. It is idolatry not less derogatory to the divine majesty and dangerous to the souls of men than the worship of Juggernaut: we use the scriptures not abuse them, but to put any thing in the place of God and pay divine honours to that thing is an abuse of it. The scripture contains a true testimony concerning the medium of revelation, but no where directs us to itself or any other book which deceitful men can expound to suit their own fancy. The word of God which liveth and abideth forever is the only safe revelation: and as to where this revelation is to be found the scriptures are sufficiently plain and explicit. 1. "The priests' lips should keep knowledge, and they should seek the law at his mouth, for he is the messenger of the lord of Hosts."[31] 2. "Know ye not that your body is the temple of God."[32] The word of God is always to be found in his temple. To Say by what miracles revelation has been in all cases confirmed is unnecessary; but that an infinity of inspirations and miracles have existed not contained in the bible, the bible itself authorises us to believe. "Many other Signs truly did Jesus in the presence of his disciples which are not written in this book."[33] "There are also many other things which Jesus did, which if they should be written every one, the world itself could not contain the book that might be written."[34] Where are all these works to be found? "He that believeth on me the works that I do shall he do also and greater."[35] Is not this proof enough of a continued revelation and a living ministry of the word? But neither will ever be found by an idolater, a lover of pleasure more than a lover of God, but the honest soul who prizes the truth above every thing else when he finds it where it is, will not try to hide himself under what Moses did write, construed to his own liking? but he of whom Moses did write becomes his confidential teacher.

Question. Do you believe that Jesus Christ is God as well as man, equal with the father, having two natures in one person? This question involves the fundamentals of the Calvinistic system, that system we do not believe, we consider the formers of it and believers in it to be no better than those learned and popular professors that Jesus Christ testified knew neither him nor his father. We are willing nevertheless to testify our faith concerning Jesus Christ and his father. But it is not what Dr. Cleland of Harrodsburg has published it to be; this calumniator would have his readers to believe that "Arians, Socinians, Swedinborgians, Universalists, Deists, Mahometans, and Shakers all associate to-

gether as members of the same family and all unite in opposing
the fundamental doctrines of christianity"[36] particularly the divinity of christ. To correct the glaring misrepresentations of this
writer whose recent works are calculated to obstruct our own
statements, we would remark that in point of either doctrine or
practice we do not associate, confederate or coalesce with any
sect or denomination of Adams posterity now living on the earth,
nor they with us; we hold ourselves as a distinct family united to
Jesus Christ as our elder brother, and of course possessing a
knowledge of his and our parents answerable to such a relation,
and of course a faith which Mahometans, Deists &c would be as
unwilling to subscribe as the above named Dr. of divinity. We
have no account that Jesus Christ ever said that he was God equal
with the father. He owned that he was the son of God. This we
believe was true. He also admitted that the father was greater
than he. This we also admit, as a son he learned obedience. This
we deem was proper for him and for us, seeing we are called to
be as he was in this world. Then "if he called them Gods to whom
the word of God came, and the scripture cannot be broken"[37] we
count it no impropriety to call him God whom the father sanctified and sent into the world, altho he was satisfied with being
esteemed a child of God. The translators of the bible say that he
"thought it not robbery to be equal with God,"[38] but the reverse
of this was written by the inspired Apostle.

Now concerning the two natures in the one person of Christ,
this we admit in the past and present time, but in relation to
futurity we reject the term *forever*. The divine and human nature
existed in the person of Christ and in all who personated him in
his first appearing. The same two natures exist in his body the
church and will continue to exist until he hath subdued all things,
and "when all things shall be subdued unto him," and the kingdom delivered up to the (father). "Then shall the son also be subject—that God may be all in all."[39]

E

A Letter from Charles Willing Byrd to William S. Byrd[40]

Sinking Spring, March 22d, 1828

Dear William,

I am favored with your letter of the 9th instant and was not a little pleased with the feeling manner in which you noticed the death of poor Lavinia.[41] When on this subject you used expressions that induce me to enquire of you, whether you believe in the salvation of all; and if you do not, whether you believe in endless punishment? If you have the least objection to making answers, you are left at perfect liberty to be silent as to both. Should you be disposed to reply to them and are at a loss in any degree, you will oblige me by consulting brother Eleazar on these topicks.

When we see each other again, it will give me pleasure and I shall feel much interest in reading the letters between our brother just named, Dr Williamson and yourself, as I did in the perusal of the first part of this correspondence; a hundred times more than from any intelligence brought by him, who "comes the herald of a noisy world, the news of all nations lumbering on his back."[42] I would be glad my son if you would shortly visit us and bring those letters with you, staying with us at least six months; and I think you ought at any rate to live half your time with me.

If Elder David[43] is still at Pleasant Hill present my love to him, to the Ministry, to brother Eleazar, and Elder brother James Congleton, for whose invitation I am very thankful. Be pleased to tell him so, and that I will avail myself of it, if I can conveniently. I sincerely regret Mother Lucys removal, and still more the cause of it.

It is satisfactory to learn from you that your health of mind and body are both better, but lament that neither the one or the other is as good as you could wish. How often and fervently have I prayed that yours and mine were entirely restored; and I cannot help still wishing that a gift of healing was imparted to some member or members of our Society for this purpose. Could this wish be realized and gratified, what a pleasing and happy confir-

113

mation would it be of the present church being the true one? As to the remarks in the Testimony on this subject that in the present works of God we are not especially at this late day to look for such things,[44] in order to induce a belief that ours is like the primitive church; when it is rememberd that in our Society at Watervliet[45] in New York those gifts have been received even within the last two years, the mind will yet dwell on the contemplation of them. I should like very much to hear or see brother Eleazars reflections on the occasion. But I charge you my William, to write only when perfectly convenient to yourself and only as much as you can pen without distressing your head; at the same time I must say that as it respects myself, you cannot write too often, as I am so much gratified to receive your letters. If the author of the Testimony is correct in his remarks on the subject, then no one of our societies had any ground to expect this miraculous gift; and those who received that gift, in considering it as a proof that we are closely allied to the primitive church, were altogether mistaken. But if these last were right in that supposition, then are we left to con-clude that our branches of that church in the Western countrey, are not the true offspring of that heavenly church, but that we are Bastards? As to your health of body and the state of your mind, I will add that you should reflect I think and perhaps you do, that if you were in the world instead of the church, you would prob-ably have the same amount and in all likelihood a greater quan-tum of disease and uneasiness than you now have. While reflect-ing on these afflictions especially of the body, which indeed have a material bearing on the mind and which undoubtedly have a tendency to make this world a hell, I will inform you of a discov-ery in diet which I have lately made, and that may be useful to you. After a full and fair trial repeated twice a day for six weeks, I find light buckwheat cakes taken quite warm with butter and coffee for breakfast and tea for dinner, to be as much lighter on the stomach, if made with good yeast, than any other bread stuff, as good venison is lighter than good beef. As to corn bread and swines flesh, they are poisonous to a weak stomach.

I have still painful apprehensions that Harmony or Busrow[46] will soon perhaps terminate Francis's earthly career: you say he is there again. It is a duty however my son, which we owe to our-selves and perhaps to God likewise, as well in relation to our own afflictions as in relation to others, to bear up against them by every manly effort we can make: always to view the best side of the question; and if it presents no good side, to think as little about it as possible. And there are some subjects independent of disease that are unpleasant, which we can work up into distress of mind, but which by a little {dexterous} management may produce a smile. For instance Powel goes contrary to my counsel in almost every thing, and avowedly so. The other day, noticing that he had recovered a state of fine health, which he was risking and abusing in various ways, and among others paying no regard to the simplicity of his solid and liquid food, and eating and drinking too much, I cautiond him in the mildest manner, telling him at the same time that the low time of provisions, even if he had not known me, would prevent a suspicion that I was desirous only to lessen the quantity of provisions consumed in the family. But as if to fulfil a threat which I think I once heard that he had ut tered, of doing a thing the sooner because I tried to dissuade him from it, he has frequently since taken two meals between breakfast and dinner. Now this extraordinary conduct of his, so far beyond what I ever dreampt of, has been a subject of laughter for Hannah and myself, and seeming that I cannot alter it by any thing I can do, I may as well smile as to lament about it until I suffer real and unavailing distress. Now I wish you my son, to borrow a hint from this, and to profit by it.

Last week I wrote to Francis. I have often sent Niles weekly Register[47] to him; and very lately forwarded one number for which I swapped another paper, of the Scioto Gazette to him, containing our New Hampshire law case, in full, with the Editors apology for delaying its publication.[48] It is a Chillicothe paper, much improved, and of a more extensive circulation I believe than any other in the state. The law case, it appeared from subsequent publications, afforded pleasure in the perusal and excited interest. I also had it inserted in the National Intelligencer,[49] a paper of a more extensive circulation through the United States than any other paper by far. It has induced the publication of a South Carolina Judges opinion in favor of admitting the evidence of a Universalist to which an objection had been raised,[50] and this without any objection being made to the decision in our case, has produced answers and replys without number.

The present appears to be an auspicious period for the safe investment of funds. Since this letter was folded up and directed a newspaper was put into my hands, shewing that "the Secretary of Pensylvania has advertized for a loan of 2,000,000$ for the railroads and canals of that State, on 5 per cent stocks; the interest to be paid semiannually, at the Treasury of the State, or the Banks of Pensylvania, at the option of the holder, and the principal at any time after Dec. 1. 1853, at the option of the State. The sum of 860,000$ will be required on the 10th of this month, and monthly installments of 190,000 on the 1st of each month from next Sept to February next."[51] This stock I think I would prefer to any other.

[*C W Byrd*]

A Letter from Charles Willing Byrd to William S. Byrd[52]

Sinking Spring, July 8, 1828

Dear William,

Brother Francis in his letter to me of the 23d of October 1827 says, "I now know a person who wishes to obtain the loan of your funds, and who proposes personal security in addition to deeds on real estate, up to my full satisfaction, which will render them safe in my estimation beyond the possibility of a doubt."[53]

I was in consequence encouraged to follow his kind advice, to authorize him to lend those funds, five thousand and ninety dollars, at lawful interest, and to take the above mentiond security. From a subsequent communication it appeard that he had effected the loan. I have since placed in his hands with the same object in view about one thousand dollars more.

In his last, under the date of the 19th of June 1828 he says, "it is impossible for any human ken to foresee what may happen, but you may rest assured, that I will deal with as much caution, or more, with your funds, than if they were my own."[54]

A recent comparison of the letters led me to the supposition, that he was not at the date of his last, so sanguine with respect to the safety of the loan, as he was at first; and that it would plead my excuse with him for making this special request, that as soon as it may be suspected that there is the most distant ground of doubt as to the sufficiency of the security, that he will immediately recover back into his own possession the whole amount, and then without loss of time make a deposit of the funds in the branch of the United States bank at Lexington. Present my love to him if you please, and name the foregoing request to him. Accept it also for yourself, for our ministry, Eleazar, brother John [Shain], and such others as it may be convenient for you to mention my name before.

The use of money I think will be in greater demand than it has been for years past. Mr. Baldwin[55] in his dinner speach at Cincinnati, the only dinner speach I ever saw that I thought worth read-

117

ing, where he was complimented with the attention of 650 sub-
scribers to the entertainment, developed in handsome colours the
rich resources of the country. His remarks seemed happily calculated to elucidate the consequences likely to result from the present tariff of 1828. While the editors of newspapers for twelve
months past have renderd the subject only more obscure, this
able lawyer has explained it in a full and satisfactory manner. In
adverting to the specious reasoning of those writers on political
economy, who for centuries have been labouring to prove the un-
sound policy of any protecting duties, he has prostrated their in-
genious arguments, by opening the book of nature, and by an ap-
peal to practical experience. He has pointed to our beds of ore,
pastures, and fields, and shewn that window glass which formerly cost fifteen dollars per box, previous to the tariff of 1824,
now costs only five.

The prevalence of the flux[56] in Ohio, induces me to repeat my
request to you, not to take any fruit at all excepting that which is
dried, and not that until it has been cooked. I learn from Mr Burgess that soda is the best preservative of the teeth.[57] A solution of
it in an ounce phial of water, putting in a small tea spoon full of
the powder, and every morning washing the teeth with about a
large tea spoonfull of the liquid, is the course he has taken with
his own for twenty years; and they are better now than they were
when he began this practise: he has every one of his teeth yet. I
mean at the age of 43 he has a full set.

Four of your cousins left us yesterday, and Tucker who is worth
all the rest of them, says he will go soon to Pleasant Hill on purpose to see you. In the best love yours,

C W Byrd

In communicating my request to brother Francis, you can you
know, shew him the letter.

Religion appears to be at a low ebb here, and preachers and
all seem to think that it consists mainly in disclaiming self righteousness and relying solely on the blood of Christ.

It is in vain for me to tell them, even to tell Mr Burges, the
cleverest of all of them, that this blood means his life, and that
the life of Christ will not save us, until we lead it ourselves.

The six thousand dollars and upwards mentiond in this letter,
are independent and exclusive of the amount heretofore vested

by brother Francis for me in the purchase of my half of McMurtry tract. He has probably told you that I entertain some hopes, being out of debt, being enabled with the interest on the money confided to his management, and with some addition that I can probably make hereafter to it, to resign my ofice in [a] year or two and live at Danville,[58] if I cannot {conveniently} get nearer to Pleasant hill.

_____ G _____

A Letter from Benjamin S. Youngs
to the Ministry at New Lebanon[59]

Confidential.

Sept. 8th. 1828.

Beloved Ministry,

I suppose it is right for me to answer your request, by sending you a few "Confidential lines" respecting the condition of P. Hill. This I suppose I might be able to do, to your satisfaction, were I really compelled to do so. But you know that confidential matters, are often very weighty, and that they are as often of as delicate a nature to meddle with, however much we may feel honestly interested or conscientiously concern'd. The condition of P. Hill is not to be despaired of, although it is indeed deplorable to what it was about five or six years ago. The Society then was strong handed, facul[t]ized,[60] industrious, wealthy and prosperous; but the concealed misery and misfortune was that they were very selfish, that they considered themselves superior in gifts and talents; in order and arrangements to any order of believers in the Western country, if not to any order of believers any where. This idea no doubt commenced at the head and pervaded the body. All applauded their Mother, as a being superior to all others on Earth. All the concerns spiritual and temporal, were almost solely in her hands, and under her personal counsel and direction. Such a state of things could not exist very many years. Elder Samuel was the first man. It was not supposed by every one that Mother knew as much about some particular kinds of business as Elder S. or even as much as many of the rest had got to know—counsels of course, became clashing, and by & by discoverable. The aspiring to Leads, and the heretical, the faultfinders and ismhunters found subjects a plenty to speculate, to reason and to debate upon. Whether in connection with these things, a selfish and craving disposition and practice, or an oppression of those in meaner circumstances, could in the course of time, have any moral tendency towards this decline among such a virtuous and prosperous people, is a question I cannot undertake to decide. In the mean

120

time there was that John Whitby in his outward appearance very mild, prudent and exemplary—but at the same time very sly, underhanded, cunning and deceitful, while at heart a perfect infidel, and secretly inculcating principles of the most dangerous and infernal kind in the most pious manner. Infidelity, pride, presumption, disorder and confusion took deep root. The contagion spread and grew into a plague. Scarcely an Elder or a Deacon but what became contaminated, or as they now call it "smoked."

"Away with the Elders and Deacons but such as are of the Peoples own choosing," became the pretty general sense; much of the private party's and some of the open conversation. "Away with the Ministry—down with priestcraft—let the people be liberated from bondage and be free to judge and to act for themselves." It is easier to sense, than it is to describe what mischief and confusion such a spirit must create. With all the labors that could be made numbers continued going off to the world leaving still their poison behind. While others as infidel as they, and who wished to be received by the body as Leads and legislators, were determind to stay on the ground, claim their right to the property and to do as they please—all this added to the distress. The Ministry had little or no power—The Elders little or no proper influence. Mother being no longer able in body or mind to bear all the distress or help the Society out of their condition, fled from the scene to Union Village—and really I think her leaving P. Hill where she had labored so faithfully for the good of the people, for so many years; cannot be considered in any other light than as a cruel banishment.

Elder Solomon [King] & others from U[nion] V[illage] staid at P. Hill from Oct. till March, Elder Eleazer & Elder David Spinning staid till summer in which as many important changes were made for the better as could be got at. The libertine spirit that seemed to be prevailing, the pride, the infidelity, the abuses, and trampling on every sacred order by the world and by apostates, & with the world—All these made it sufficiently evident that the Society were in a rapid way to ruin. The sincere and thinking part, could not but feel troubled—others also became convicted of the necessity of a reform. Many came to confession and manifested strong desires for a change. But here again was the mischief; not one out of ten perhaps, after a private confession, would come boldly and openly forward and declare their determination for the gospel, and openly renounce their former spirit and ways. In this manner the better part could gain but little strength while the opposite parties could see their weakness and still take encouragement in rebellion and find support for their hopes for yet gaining the objects of their vain and wild pursuits.

It was some encouraging, however, that towards the latter part of those distressing scenes, the good spirit seemed to be gaining ground—most of the greatest infidels and mischief makers were purged out, and those who remained, seemed to find themselves weakened and disappointed, while the principal members, and Society in general seemed interested and intent on being awake & alive to their union and interest in the Gospel.

Thus far I have stated in pretty general terms, and I think pretty correctly the condition of P. Hill, say for about two years preceeding this summer past. Last winter the apostates having got a law[61] past against the Believers, it was concluded best to remonstrate against it by a publication to the political world. This publication was so strenuously opposed by certain of those libertine characters at P. Hill whose determination was that nothing should be done but by their vote or rather by their will & direction nothing could be done in it—indeed they wished apostates & enemies good success—they wished to see the Society fall and be broken to pieces in order that they might be built up and in wanton on its ruins! In the "name of the Lord Jesus and Mother Ann!" and there was not energy nor strength of union enough in the Society to determine the publication. These difficulties were the principal cause of my going to P. Hill which I was there in May and June. Letter after letter came forward full of blind matter, pious infidelity and reasoning opposition against the propriety of publishing anything more to the world. To these letters we made no replies—but publicly and privately used our best wisdom & exertions, to gain and collect together the general and principal union of the Society, and in such a manner that none could oppose without making it manifest to all that they were in direct opposition to the gospel.

It was plainly manifest that unless we published whatever we thought best to be published on the present occasion, the designing spirits of opposition would have claimed the day, and the Society as an orderly body of Believers might begin to bid adieu to all their remaining power and prosperity. The work proceeded, was printed and published as you see it.[62] It has met with no open (if any) opposition that we know of, and we had reason to believe that it would essentially strengthen the union and interested feelings of the Society generally, while it would weaken the progress of the evil. As to the effect the late law will have on the property of the Believers in this State (Ky) we cannot certainly tell, as it has not as yet come to sufficient trial—but we have not as yet had sufficient reason to apprehend any sudden danger. The lawyers and Judges who have read our publication are much pleased with it, and say that the turbulent spirits may be at rest.

You wished to know whether South Union were likely to be effected by the difficulties at P.H? To which we answer that the contagion was too deeply rooted, and too general both at the Hill & Bussrow also, for South Union & even Union Village not to be more or less effected by it. It was from a knowledge of this fact, that while on our way to the East the Spring before last, we particularly requested both at P. Hill and U. Village not to have any visits made to S. Union during our absence. But so it was; Visits were made in our absence to our labor and sorrow. In the breaking up of Bussrow, there were some apostates left behind who corresponded with the unsteady ones of other places; and some unsettled wandering Stars who first went about from place to place among Believers so as to be [able] to choose a home to suit themselves. Among this latter class was one Daniel Rankin[63] a proud unmortified self important Dandy. First he went to Watervliet in O. next to Union Village—then away to P. Hill where he put up for seven months, and professed to have found a most happy home.

This same Daniel Rankin after sending much vile stuff & poison to his Bussrow acquaintances at South Union, by writing and making appointments by writing with the Apostates at Bussrow to meet him at S. Union. Starts from P. Hill some time in Aug. (I think) and brings with him a corrupt and rotton hearted man by the name of Robert Barnett[64] on a visit to South Union. These together with the infidel apostate Richardson Whitby,[65] brother to that John Whitby all come puffed up with new discoveries of light and knowledge & full of ministrations, commissions from the school of infidel philosophy and corruption at P. H. They spent as much time here as they pleased, and did as much mischief in secret as they could—left their poison and returned to their places. It is not necessary to inform you the particular effects from the influence of these vile men.

Suffice it to say we found the sense of some changed from better to worse. It cost us considerable labor and sorrow. Some went to the world, and others by much labor and patience have been thus far saved like brands plucked out of the burning. Upon the whole we have not suffered more than what we had calculated upon, and we are in hopes that the Society will suffer no very serious or irrecoverable loss—as general good union prevails, and infidelity is little countenanced or talked of.

Benjamin S. Y.

The Last Will and Testament
of William S. Byrd[66]

I William S Byrd, of Pleasant Hill, in Mercer County, State of
Kentucky, being of sound and disposing mind and memory, do
make and ordain this my last will and testament, in the form
following, (To Wit,)—I give & bequeath to Abram Wilhite[67] and
Francis Voris my moiety or half part of the tract of land of about
two hundred and forty eight acres purchased by my father and
myself of William McMurtry, in Mercer County and State aforesaid. I do also give to the said Abram and Francis the whole of my
Dismal Swamp stock in the State of Virginia, being five shares.
And I further will and give unto the said Abram & Francis, the lot
of four acres of ground in Adams County, Ohio, willed to me by
my father;[68] and also my right to the remainder of five hundred
dollars, in the hands of John Page,[69] in Frederick County Virginia,
the present use for life was given to my sister Molly Randolph. I
also will and bequeath to the said Abram and Francis all my remainder to a certain family of negroes,[70] at present in the occu-
pation and possession of my grandfather Col. Meade of Jessamine
County, with power to emancipate any slave or slaves that may
fall into their hands through me. I also will & bequeath unto the
said Abram & Francis all moneys, bonds, accounts, *or choses in
action* that I may in any way or manner, be entitled to as one of
the heirs and devisees of Charles W. Byrd deceased, or any other
person within revision or in remainder, or any other way, or manner whatsoever. The whole to be used and held by them, in trust,
for the use and benefit of the Society of people called Shakers, at
Pleasant Hill, in Mercer County and State of Kentucky, with
power to sell or dispose of, and make good titles to any or all of it
so sold; and for them to use the proceeds as aforesaid. And lastly,
I appoint the said Abram Wilhite and Francis Voris my Executors
to this my last Will and Testament, requesting the County Court
to dispense with the ordinary forms of bond and security, as my
will is that no bond or security shall be required of them. Wholly
written with my own hand. In testimony whereof I have hereunto

set my hand and affixed my seal at Pleasant Hill, this 4th day of November, in the year of our Lord 1828.

William S. Byrd

C. R. Lewis[71]
Brice Bradshaw[72]
Leonard Jones

A Spirit Letter from William S. Byrd
To Martin Runyon[73]

Pleasant Hil Ky. Wednesday, July 29th, 1840,
First Order. A Letter from William Byrd
(a faithful young believer),
to Martin Runyon, read by Katharine McCullough,
an inspired instrument.

Beloved brother Martin,

In union with our blessed Mother [Ann Lee], I now have this opportunity to converse with you by way of letter. It is a great and glorious privilege, one that I prize more than all earthly enjoyments. Now my beloved brother, you know while on earth I lived, I was called by the sounding trumpet of God, to arise and flee from Sodom, to give up all earthly enjoyments for my salvation. This I done according to my understanding. And O! I give praise and glory to God, that I was called by the sounding trumpet, so that I might find a place in the kingdom of heaven. Now my brother, you know I was like a falling leaf, or fading flower, that bloomed to last but a short time. I was touched with the cold hand of death, and my precious Mother said to me, "Come my little child, your time on earth is done." After I laid down this tabernacle, the holy Angels guarded me, and took me to the mansions of Charity; and my heavenly Father said to me, "Come in, come in, my child, here is a work for you to do." He gave me a little book, and said, "Here, look therein, and ye will find what to do," and O! how thankful I felt, that I had a kind Father & Mother to protect me; and that I had found the way to purge and purify my soul, and make it clean and white. Yea I passed through the refiners fire, I here confessed all the wrongs that I had committed during my life. My precious Mother then said to me, "you have done this work faithfully, you can now rejoice in the way of God, and be exceeding glad." And here were four thousand holy angels, who accompanied me to the white plains, where we sang heavenly praises, and give glory to God Almighty, for the way of salvation, which I have gained by the cross and by selfdenial. My precious Mother said to me, "My child, you look pure and white, and as unfettered as a little dove." This word I prized more than all the riches and honors of this transient world; for I say unto you, the rich, the high and lofty, will have to bow low, low to the dust, if ever they find salvation. Now beloved brother, precious Mother says, you have waded through deep tribulation, you have suffered and toiled for your salvation. You forsook your house and land, your wife, and children for my sake, and the kingdom of heaven, saith the Lord, and great will be your reward in the kingdom, if ye will persevere, and hold out to the end; for I say unto you, there is none that enters the kingdom, only by the cross of Christ: it is none, saith the Lord, but these who are willing to give up all, the world, flesh and devil, who are willing to bow low, low, and humble themselves in true submission, before the Lord God, and his heavenly train. Beloved brother, precious Mother says, you have a right to rejoice and be glad, that the great day of redemption has come. Now Brother, I have a present for thee, it is a golden box filled with the true substance of the gospel, for you to keep, in remembrance of me, in your more declining years. Now my brother, precious Mother says, if ye will bear the cross of true selfdenial, I will help you through each trying hour, and you shall sit beneath my bower, low, low, in the mansions of peace. These are the words of your Heavenly Mother. Now here is a present from Father William[74] to you, it is a twig of the great union tree, and it is full of little birds, and you must shake this twig; and there is a Bird for every one, their names are prayerfulness; for I say unto you, souls will have to learn to be prayerful, and watchful, lest the enemy should steal away their treasures. It is none but the meek, the low, and honest hearted that will in the gospel thrive and grow.

　　Now my brother, since I laid down my body, I have seen souls drop into eternity, who were loaded with sins and abominations, who wickedly and wilfully rejected this gospel, who hardened their hearts, and turned a deaf ear, these are the ones that sink into that awful gulf, which separates them from God and happiness. I have seen none of this number, who have ever returned. And I do solemnly warn all, both great and small, to walk low and humble, to bear the cross of true selfdenial against all that is unclean, and contrary to this gospel; for souls who will wither and die in these enlightened days, will have to give an account of all the time they have misspent.

Now my brother, I thank you for your unwearied pains during my illness, I was a poor suffering mortal, but now I do not suffer, that old body has turned into dust. Now I will draw to a close, by sending you my kind love and blessing, in twelve low bows, to the Ministry, Elders, brethren and sisters. So fare ye well, with my kind and everlasting love.

Martin Runyon.   *William Byrd.*

NOTES

ABBREVIATIONS

CWB	Charles Willing Byrd
FC	Manuscript Collections, Filson Club, Louisville, Kentucky
LC	Shaker Papers, Library of Congress, Washington, D.C.
LLIU	Byrd Papers, Lilly Library, Indiana University, Bloomington, Indiana
MCHS	Shaker Papers, Mercer County Historical Society, Harrodsburg, Kentucky
OHS	Manuscript Collections, Ohio Historical Society, Columbus, Ohio
RCHS	Byrd Papers, Ross County Historical Society, Chillicothe, Ohio
SPH	Shaker Papers, Shakertown at Pleasant Hill, Kentucky
KLUK	Manuscript Collections, M.I. King Library, University of Kentucky, Lexington, Kentucky
WRHS	Shaker Papers, Western Reserve Historical Society, Cleveland, Ohio
WSB	William S. Byrd

INTRODUCTION

1. Ministry, Pleasant Hill, to Ministry, New Lebanon, New York, Aug. 1, 1826 (WRHS). For a description of conditions in western Shakerism at the time, see F. Gerald Ham, "Shakerism in the Old West" (Ph.D. diss., Univ. of Kentucky, 1962).

2. Ministry, Pleasant Hill, to Ministry, New Lebanon, Aug. 1 and 12, 1825, and Aug. 1, 1826 (WRHS). On the Byrd family, see

Marion Tinling, ed., *The Correspondence of the Three William Byrds of Westover, Virginia, 1684-1776*, 2 vols. (Charlottesville, Va., 1977). CWB's life is described in Nelson W. Evans and Emmons B. Stivers, *A History of Adams County, Ohio* (West Union, Ohio, 1900), pp. 526-32; W.H. Burtner, Jr., "Charles Willing Byrd," *Ohio Archaeological and Historical Quarterly* 41 (1932): 237-40; Gerald J. Geiger, "Charles Willing Byrd" (M.A. thesis, Indiana Univ., 1951); and Stephen J. Stein, "The Conversion of Charles Willing Byrd to Shakerism," *Filson Club History Quarterly* 56 (1982): 395-414. In *The Shaker Spiritual* (Princeton, N.J., 1979), Daniel W. Patterson identifies CWB as an exceptional convert because of his wealth (p. 177).

3. No critical history of Pleasant Hill exists at present. Nevertheless, the following are useful: Thomas D. Clark and F. Gerald Ham, *Pleasant Hill and Its Shakers* (Pleasant Hill, Ky., 1968); Samuel Thomas and James Thomas, *The Simple Spirit: A Pictorial History of Pleasant Hill* (Pleasant Hill, Ky., 1973); Samuel W. Thomas and Mary Lawrence Young, "The Development of Shakertown at Pleasant Hill, Kentucky," *Filson Club History Quarterly* 49 (1975): 231-55; and Julia Neal, *The Kentucky Shakers* (Lexington, Ky., 1977).

4. In the Shaker tradition, "bearing the cross" referred specifically to the practice of celibacy prescribed by the founder Ann Lee.

5. For a general account of the religious history of the United States during the antebellum period, see Sydney E. Ahlstrom, *A Religious History of the American People* (New Haven, Conn., 1972), especially pp. 385-729.

6. The relationship between Shakerism and western revivalism is described in Richard McNemar, *The Kentucky Revival, or, A Short History of the Late Extraordinary Out-Pouring of the Spirit of God, in the Western States of America, Agreeably to Scripture-Promises, and Prophecies concerning the Latter Day: with a Brief Account of the Entrance and Progress of What the World call Shakerism, Among the Subjects of the Late Revival in Ohio and Kentucky* (Cincinnati, 1807), especially pp. 79-115; J.P. MacLean, "The Kentucky Revival and Its Influence on the Miami Valley," *Shakers of Ohio: Fugitive Papers Concerning the Shakers of Ohio, With Unpublished Manuscripts* (Columbus, Ohio, 1907), pp. 19-58; Ham, "Shakerism," especially chapter 1; John B. Boles, *The Great Re-*

vival, 1787-1805: The Origins of the Southern Evangelical Mind (Lexington, Ky., 1972), pp. 156-58; and Neal, *Kentucky Shakers,* pp. 1-11. The situation at South Union is depicted in Julia Neal, *By Their Fruits: The Story of Shakerism in South Union, Kentucky* (Chapel Hill, N.C., 1947).

7. John McKelvie Whitworth, *God's Blueprint: A Sociological Study of Three Utopian Sects* (London, 1975), p. 49. Deprivation theory also informs the judgments of D'Ann Campbell, "Women's Life in Utopia: The Shaker Experiment in Sexual Equality Reappraised—1810 to 1860," *New England Quarterly* 51 (1978): 23-38; Lawrence Foster, *Religion and Sexuality: Three American Communal Experiments of the Nineteenth Century* (New York, 1981), especially pp. 48-58; and William Sims Bainbridge, "Shaker Demographics, 1840-1900: An Example of the Use of U.S. Census Enumeration Schedules," *Journal for the Scientific Study of Religion* 21 (1982): 352-65.

8. Stephen A. Marini, *Radical Sects of Revolutionary New England* (Cambridge, Mass., 1982), p. 96.

9. Ministry, Pleasant Hill, to Ministry, New Lebanon, Apr. 12, 1825, and Aug. 1, 1826 (WRHS).

10. For a biography of William Byrd II, see Pierre Marambaud, *William Byrd of Westover, 1674-1744* (Charlottesville, Va., 1971). Michael Zuckerman provides an insightful analysis of Byrd's private and public life in "William Byrd's Family," *Perspectives in American History,* ed. Donald Fleming, 12 (1979): 255-311. The genteel quality of Byrd family life is described in Philip Greven, *The Protestant Temperament: Patterns of Child-Rearing, Religious Experience, and the Self in Early America* (New York, 1977), especially pp. 263-331; and Louis B. Wright, *The First Gentlemen of Virginia: Intellectual Qualities of the Early Colonial Ruling Class* (Charlottesville, Va., 1940), pp. 312-47. For a biography of William Byrd III, see Tinling, *Correspondence,* 2: 604-14. CWB's relatively small inheritance is documented in "The Will of William Byrd III," in "Letters of the Byrd Family," *Virginia Magazine of History and Biography* 38 (1930): 59-63; and "The Will of Mrs. Mary Willing Byrd, of Westover, 1813, with a List of the Westover Portraits," *Virginia Magazine of History and Biography* 6 (1899): 346-58.

11. CWB, "Diary" no. 5, Jan. 1824, p. 12 (RCHS). Five unnumbered and undated manuscript diaries exist among CWB's papers

at the RCHS. Numbers have been supplied for the diaries by the author.

12. CWB's family and influential friends in Philadelphia proved instrumental in his rising fortunes. Concerning his mother's relatives, see Burton Alva Konkle, *Thomas Willing and the First American Financial System* (Philadelphia, 1937). CWB studied law with Gouverneur Morris and subsequently became the western agent of the financier Robert Morris. Byrd became a member of the Jeffersonian "Virginia junta" of Ross County, Ohio. CWB's role in the politics of the Northwest Territory is apparent from his letter to Thomas Jefferson, Oct. 15, 1802, cited in Randolph Chandler Downes, "Thomas Jefferson and the Removal of Governor St. Clair in 1802," *Ohio State Archaeological and Historical Quarterly* 36 (1927): 73-74; and from David Meade Massie, *Nathaniel Massie, a Pioneer of Ohio* (Cincinnati, 1896). On Sarah Meade's background, see "Meade Family History," *William and Mary Quarterly*, 1st ser., 13 (1904): 37; and Henry J. Peet, ed., *Chaumiere Papers, Containing Matters of Interest to the Descendants of David Meade, of Nansemond County, Va., Who died in the year 1757* (Chicago, 1883). For a description of the lavish circumstances at Chaumiere, see Bennett H. Young, *A History of Jessamine County, Kentucky, from its Earliest Settlement to 1898* (Louisville, Ky., 1898), pp. 215-19; Ida Withers Harrison, "Chaumiere du Prairie," *Journal of American History* 9 (1915): 563-73; and *Survey of Historic Sites in Kentucky: Jessamine County* (Frankfort, Ky., 1979), pp. 112-15. Family influence was probably responsible for Byrd's appointment to the federal court. His aunt in Philadelphia told of her efforts on his behalf (Elizabeth Powel to CWB, Feb. 28, 1800 [LLIU]). Several years earlier Thomas Willing had sent $500 to CWB for assistance in purchasing a farm in Kentucky. See Thomas Willing to CWB, Oct. 16, 1794 (LLIU).

13. Thomas W. Francis to CWB, Aug. 2, 1798 (LLIU); CWB to Nathaniel Massie, June 20, 1802 (Meade, *Nathaniel Massie*, pp. 210-11); to Evelyn Harrison, Feb. 17, 1806, and May 25, 1815 (LLIU); to David Meade, Mar. 2, 1815 (LLIU); and to WSB, Mar. 22, 1828 (LLIU) (See Appendix E, herein.) Concerning the "system of supercharged sociability," including "incessant visiting," that characterized the life of Virginia planters, see Zuckerman, "William Byrd's Family," pp. 288-97; Rhys Isaac, *The Transformation of Virginia, 1740-1790* (Chapel Hill, N.C., 1982), especially pp. 58-

87; and Jan Lewis, *The Pursuit of Happiness: Family and Values in Jefferson's Virginia* (Cambridge, Eng., 1983), pp. 22-24. The book *Trifles for Children*, part II (Philadelphia, 1809), is signed in the childhood hand of Kidder M. Byrd (LLIU).

14. WSB's middle name is most unusual in view of the names given to his siblings. In the manuscripts it is spelled variously, including "Siloue," and "Siloe." The name ties WSB to his grandfather's exploits. In 1760, while on a business expedition, William Byrd III fell into the hands of an unfriendly group of Cherokee Indians, who were upset by recent losses in warfare. When it was decided to avenge the losses by killing Byrd, one of the Cherokees named Silouee intervened physically, calling Byrd his friend and brother. This episode is cited by Thomas Jefferson in *Notes on the State of Virginia* (Paris, 1785), p. 109. For more details on the story, see Samuel G. Drake, *The Book of the Indians of North America*, 11th ed. (Boston, 1851), pp. 378-79.

15. Mary Willing Byrd to CWB, June 27, 1811, July 11, 1812, and June 1813; and to Mary Willing (Molly) Byrd, Aug. 17, 1811; John Richard to CWB, May 30, 1813 (all in LLIU).

16. Among CWB's diaries is an entry itemizing fees for tuition ("Diary" no. 5, p. 6 [RCHS]). Kidder's unsuccessful efforts to find gainful employment as a lawyer are described in his letter to WSB, Sept. 6, 1824 (LLIU). WSB's own knowledge of the law is apparent in several letters (see herein those of June 22 and July 13, 1826). WSB had studied law, for Kidder addressed his letter to "William S Byrd Esquire, Student at law, Sinking Spring, Highland County, State of Ohio."

17. William Byrd II described the Dismal Swamp in a letter to Charles Boyle, May 27, 1728 (Tinling, *Correspondence*, 1:373-74); and in a posthumous publication entitled "A Description of the Dismal Swamp, in Virginia; with Proposals for and Observations on the Advantages of Draining it," *Universal Asylum and Columbian Magazine* 3 (1789): 230-34. See Peter C. Stewart, "Man and the Swamp: The Historical Dimension," in *The Great Dismal Swamp*, ed. Paul W. Kirk, Jr. (Charlottesville, Va., 1979), pp. 57-73. William Byrd II, along with George Washington and others, had a hand in forming the Dismal Swamp Land Company, which engaged in a number of speculative and investment schemes. WSB received $222.95 in dividends from his shares between 1818 and 1827.

18. Marambaud, *William Byrd*, p. 61; Tinling, *Correspondence*, 2:613. The piety of the Byrd women is apparent in letters from Mary Willing Byrd to CWB, June 27 and Aug. 17, 1811; Evelyn Harrison to CWB, May 25, 1815, and Jan. 1, 1816; and Maria Page to CWB, Dec. 23, 1817 (all in LLIU).

19. See CWB to Richard Byrd, Feb. 3, 1815 (OHS). For a fuller discussion of CWB's religious development, see Stein, "Conversion."

20. CWB, "Abridgment of My Advice to My Children on Some Important Subjects. July 21, 1821" (RCHS), pp. 1, 3-4.

21. John McLean to CWB, Oct. 9, 1824; CWB to John W. Campbell, Feb. 3, 1826; and to Kidder Meade Byrd, Feb. 28, 1821, and Sept. 22, 1824 (all in LLIU); CWB, "Diary" no. 1, p. 34; no. 4, p. 24; and no. 5, pp. 5, 15, and 36 (RCHS). See also Kidder Meade Byrd's letters to CWB, June 10, July 18, and Aug. 24, 1820; and to WSB, Sept. 24, 1824 (all in LLIU).

22. Ministry, Pleasant Hill, to Ministry, New Lebanon, Aug. 1 and Aug. 12, 1825; and Aug. 1, 1826. Youngs' volume, *The Testimony of Christ's Second Appearing Containing a General Statement of All Things Pertaining to the Faith and Practice of the Church of God in this Latter-day* (Union Village, Ohio, 1808), called by some the "Shaker Bible," went through four editions before the Civil War. For details concerning its editions, see Mary L. Richmond, *Shaker Literature: A Bibliography*, 2 vols. (Hancock, Mass., 1977), 1: 211-14. Citations of the *Testimony* in this book are from the third edition (Union Village, Ohio, 1823). Edward Deming Andrews offers the judgment concerning the *Testimony* in *The People Called Shakers: A Search for the Perfect Society* (New York, 1963), p. 95. Dunlavy's *The Manifesto, or a Declaration of the Doctrines and Practice of the Church of Christ* (Pleasant Hill, Ky., 1818) also became a standard exposition of Shakerism. See Richmond, *Shaker Literature*, 1: 72-73. CWB's list of questions for the Shakers (Appendix A herein) signals the most pressing religious issues for him. It also provides a measure of the religious context in which WSB came to manhood.

23. Ministry, Pleasant Hill to Ministry, New Lebanon, Aug. 1, 1826 (WRHS); CWB, "Diary" no. 1, p. 34 (RCHS); CWB, "Abridgment of My Advice," p. 23. See also CWB's list of "Proofs that the Believers, called Shakers, are the Church of Christ" ("Diary" no. 1, p. 15).

24. Williamson served as the Presbyterian minister at West Union, Ohio, from 1805 to 1819. Burgess, who had a reputation for both religious and medical knowledge, succeeded him in that position from 1820 to 1829. See Evans and Stivers, *History of Adams County*, pp. 514-21, 634-37. See CWB to William Williamson, May 8, 1826 (LLIU); and CWB, "Diary" no. 1, p. 34 (RCHS). CWB described Burgess as "a highly respectable Presbyterian minister of the Gospel" ("Diary" no. 2, p. 9). CWB's religious counsel to his children in 1826 included the following: "Religion—on this all important subject, ask instruction of the United Society called Shakers—read the Testimony of Christs second appearing three times attentively over, and form as close an intimacy with them as you possibly can" ("Abridgment of My Advice," p. 23).

25. CWB to William Williamson, June 7, 1826 (LLIU).

26. Ministry, Pleasant Hill to Ministry, New Lebanon, Aug. 1, 1826 (WRHS). CWB, "Objections and obstacles in the way of a removal into the Society of Believers" and "Considerations in favor of a removal into the Society of Believers" ("Diary" no. 1, pp. 11-12) [RCHS].

27. See Thomas and Thomas, *Simple Spirit*, especially pp. 16-20. The meetinghouse provided a large area free of obstructions for accommodating the Shaker dances. The building, measuring 60 × 44 feet, rests "upon a heavy limestone foundation." The roof and ceiling are "suspended on a series of interlocking cantilever-type trusses and overhead studdings and rafters." The weight is distributed by means of "ceiling cross beams" and "tie trusses." See Clark and Ham, *Pleasant Hill*, pp. 17-19.

28. In his letters WSB provided information concerning the activities of the ministry at the village and the leaders of the First Order (i.e., the Church) and the East Family. He was also closely involved with the trustees of the community.

29. "Letters on the Condition of Kentucky, No. 7," *Richmond Enquirer*, May 3, 1825, p. 3.

30. See (herein) WSB to CWB, June 22, and July 13, 1826. See also Francis Voris to CWB, Sept. 16, 1826 (LLIU), in Appendix B, in which details of the potential purchase are discussed at length.

31. Health is a specific topic in the following letters of WSB to CWB (herein): June 22, July 13, and Dec. 29, 1826; May 25, 1827; and Mar. 9, Apr. 13, May 18, and June 19, 1828. CWB's diaries are filled with observations and remedies bearing on various ills. The

recommendations for WSB are in "Diary" no. 3, p. 17 (RCHS), and in MS Notes, no date (LLIU). CWB recorded the following on June 30, 1826: "In consequence I believe of taking once in three nights, a blue pill, the intestinal canal has been weakened by too frequent a discharge, and a severe cramp in the feet, legs, and ankels have been caused" ("Diary" no. 1, p. 8). "Warm bath—most highly recommended especially to such invalids as myself" ("Diary" no. 2, p. 15). "Quacks and Patent medicines to be taken internally, are I believe all of them injurious" ("Diary" no. 4, p. 10). Among CWB's papers is a series of eight letters (LLIU) written by Jasper Hand, a physician at Hillsboro, Ohio, over a period of three months during 1826-1827. Hand directs his comments to CWB's symptoms.

32. In his advice to his children, CWB declared that a "healthy residence, temperance, and exercise" are "essential" to the preservation of health ("Abridgment of My Advice," p. 1). WSB discusses his problems with the stove in his letters to CWB (herein) of Nov. 28, 1826, and Jan. 25 and Feb. 25, 1827. The topic of physical activity appears in WSB to CWB (herein), June 22, 1826, and Aug. 20, 1827. In September 1826 WSB purchased a "Testament," according to the village account book. The following June he paid $1.62 for "one octavo Bible." See "Account Book B, sales and purchases 1826-1830" (FC), pp. 51, 95.

33. CWB visited Pleasant Hill at least three times within a period of fifteen months: fall 1826, spring 1827, and late summer 1827. See (herein) WSB to CWB, July 13 and Dec. 29, 1826, and May 25, July 24, and Aug. 20, 1827. WSB's contacts with his relatives in Kentucky are noted in WSB to CWB, Dec. 29, 1826, and Jan. 25 and Apr. 11, 1827.

34. Voris assisted WSB in securing a bureau, leggings, and possibly a stove. See (herein) WSB to CWB, Nov. 28 and Dec. 29, 1826. According to a ledger entry dated Oct. 26, 1826, WSB paid ten dollars for "One Beauro" and one additional dollar for a "Mounting for same." See "Account Book B," p. 57 (FC). During the first six months of his stay at Pleasant Hill WSB also bought a brush, pantaloons, mittens, a hat, buttons, and several varieties of cloth (flannel, cashmere, bombazette, and holland) for making other items of clothing.

35. See (herein) WSB to CWB, Nov. 28, 1826. In addition to the discussions concerning sickness and health in WSB's letters (see

note 31), descriptions of WSB's physical and mental condition are contained in Francis Voris to CWB, Sept. 16, 1826, and Oct. 23, 1827 (LLIU); and Leonard Jones to CWB, Feb. 4 and Apr. 12, 1827 (LLIU).

36. WSB and CWB together paid $2,060 for the acreage. See Appendix C (herein) for the deed and details of the transaction. The continuing conflict over the purchase is evident in WSB to CWB, Dec. 29, 1826, Nov. 11, 1827, and July 14, 1828 (herein); and in CWB to WSB, July 8, 1828 (Appendix F herein). See also "Account Book B," pp. 33-34, 51-52, 95-96, and 156-57 (FC), for further details concerning WSB's account at the village; the entries for CWB are on pp. 35-36.

37. See (herein) WSB to CWB, Jan. 25, 1827. The ministry at Pleasant Hill earlier had discussed the problem of courting wealthy potential converts. See Mother Lucy Smith to Ministry, New Lebanon, May 1, 1823 (WRHS). She described a situation in which the Believers were accused of trying "to hold" a young man's "property."

38. See (herein) WSB to CWB, Feb. 25, 1827. The ministry's assurances concerning privacy are described in WSB to CWB, Jan. 25, 1827 (herein). The usefulness of WSB's correspondence from the standpoint of the ministry is apparent in his letter to Doctor Williamson, Oct. 28, 1827 (Appendix D herein). WSB purchased an inkstand in September 1826 ("Account Book B," p. 51 [FC]).

39. WSB's correspondence with his sisters is cited herein in his letters to CWB, Nov. 28, 1826, and Feb. 25, Apr. 11, July 31, and Nov. 11, 1827. WSB also corresponded with relatives at Chaumiere, as is evident from his letter to CWB, Dec. 29, 1826. CWB's disciplinary pattern and problems are apparent in "Diary" no. 3, p. 5 (RCHS); "Diary" no. 1, pp. 6, 28; "Diary" no. 5, pp. 15, 37–38; CWB to Kidder Byrd, Feb. 28, 1821 (LLIU); and to WSB, Mar. 22, 1828 (Appendix E herein). A negative response to CWB's conversion to Shakerism is expressed in Evelyn Byrd to CWB, Feb. 6, 1828 (LLIU).

40. WSB to CWB (herein), July 13, 1826, and Jan. 25, Feb. 25, Apr. 11, mid-May, and May 25, 1827; and Leonard Jones to CWB, Feb. 4 and Apr. 12, 1827 (LLIU). See Ministry, Pleasant Hill, to Ministry, New Lebanon, May 7, 1823, and Apr. 12, 1825 (WRHS), concerning Jones, who apparently assisted the village trustees on

more than one occasion. On Nov. 4, 1828, Jones was one of three witnesses to the filing of WSB's will. Earlier the same year, WSB had served as a witness in company with Richard McNemar to the formal release and transfer of all claims by William Bryant ("Church Record Book B" [MCHS], pp. 30-31). Concerning the occurrence of visions at Pleasant Hill in the 1820s, see a letter from Samuel Turner to Calvin Green at New Lebanon, Apr. 26, 1827 (LC).

41. WSB to CWB (herein), Nov. 28 and Dec. 29, 1826, and Feb. 25 and Apr. 11, 1827. There is no adequate historical account of the Shaker village at Busro Creek on the Wabash River in Indiana which began in 1810 and collapsed in 1827. Its inhabitants were dispersed to other western villages, including Pleasant Hill. See Oliver W. Robinson, "The Shakers in Knox County," *Indiana Magazine of History* 30 (1938): 34-41. A group of letters from Busro has been collected among the Shaker papers at WRHS. The most useful description of West Union is found in John McLean, "Shakers of Eagle and Straight Creeks," *Shakers of Ohio*, pp. 270-346, which contains village records.

42. Whitbey read Robert Owen's *New View of Society* (London, 1818). See Ham, "Shakerism," pp. 182-87; and Whitbey, *Beauties of Priestcraft* (New Harmony, Ind., 1826). Benjamin S. Youngs gave a detailed account of the problems at Pleasant Hill in a letter to the Ministry at New Lebanon, Sept. 8, 1828 (Appendix G herein).

43. WSB to CWB (herein), May 25, 1827, and Mar. 9, 1828. Elder Samuel Turner also kept track of the arrivals in his personal diary; see Turner, "Early Records of Pleasant Hill, Feb. 19, 1806-1836" (SPH), pp. 12-13.

44. See (herein) WSB to CWB, May 25, July 24, and July 31, 1827.

45. See (herein) WSB to CWB, July 31, 1827, and Mar. 9, 1828.

46. See (herein) WSB to CWB, Mar. 9, 1828. Mother Lucy Smith left Pleasant Hill on Nov. 19, 1827. Following her departure, Elder Samuel Turner became first in the ministry. In his private journal, Turner made the following entry: "November 19th 1827   Mother Lucy, Betsy Wilhite, in company with Thankful Thomas, started for U. Village Expecting to winter there." See Turner, "Early Records," p. 12. Ham concludes that the basic reason for Mother Lucy's removal was incompetence and her inabil-

ity to lead effectively ("Shakerism," pp. 181-87). WSB and CWB remained personally attached to her; see CWB to WSB, Mar. 22, 1828 (Appendix E herein); and WSB to CWB, June 19, 1828.

47. See WSB to CWB (herein), June 19, 1828; Ministry, Pleasant Hill, to Ministry, New Lebanon, June 28, 1828 (WRHS).

48. See WSB to CWB (herein), Feb. 25 and July 31, 1827, and June 19, 1828. See also "Gass and Bonta against Wilhite and Others—a society of Shakers" in James G. Dana, ed., *Reports of Selected Cases Decided in the Court of Appeals of Kentucky During the Year 1834* (Louisville, Ky., 1899), 2: 170-203. See also Andrews, *People Called Shakers*, pp. 204-7; and Carol Weisbrod, *The Boundaries of Utopia* (New York, 1980), especially pp. 133-34.

49. Benjamin S. Youngs to the Ministry, New Lebanon, Sept. 8, 1828 (Appendix G herein). An earlier description of the conflict at Pleasant Hill is found in Solomon King's letter to the Ministry, New Lebanon, Feb. 14, 1828 (WRHS).

50. Youngs to the Ministry, New Lebanon, Sept. 8, 1828.

51. Youngs, ibid., and letter to Amos and Chancey, Sept. 12, 1829 (WRHS). The Shaker defense of their position was published in *Investigator, or A Defense of the Order, Government & Economy of the United Society called Shakers, Against Sundry Charges & Legislative Proceedings. Addressed to the Political World* (Lexington, Ky., 1828). Later they also published *A Memorial Remonstrating Against a Certain Act of the Legislature of Kentucky* (Harrodsburg, Ky., 1830), of which McNemar was again the principal author. WSB describes his declining health in letters to CWB of May 18 and June 19, 1828.

52. WSB's increasing self-confidence as an apologist for Shaker beliefs is evident in his letters to CWB of Mar. 9 and Apr. 13, 1828. The western experience of the Shakers proved highly conducive to creative theological reflection. One recent attempt to describe Shaker theology and spirituality is Robley Edward Whitson, ed., *The Shakers: Two Centuries of Spiritual Reflection* (New York, 1983).

53. See (herein) WSB to CWB, May 25, 1827.

54. Youngs, *Testimony*, pp. 410-13.

55. Dunlavy, *Manifesto*, p. 269; and WSB to CWB (herein), Nov. 28, 1826, and Mar. 9 and May 18, 1828.

56. Dunlavy, *Manifesto*, pp. 296, 317; WSB to CWB (herein), Mar. 9, 1828; and CWB, "Diary" no. 1, pp. 15, 31 (RCHS).

57. See (herein) WSB to CWB, May 25, 1827, and Mar. 9 and June 19, 1828.

58. See (herein) WSB to CWB, Aug. 20, 1827; and Dunlavy, *Manifesto*, pp. 286, 291.

59. See (herein) WSB to CWB, Dec. 29, 1826, and Aug. 20 and Nov. 11, 1827.

60. Youngs, *Testimony*, p. 475; WSB to CWB (herein), July 13, 1826; and CWB, "Questions to Believers" (Appendix A).

61. See (herein) WSB to CWB, Mar. 9, 1828.

62. See (herein) WSB to CWB, July 14, 1828; CWB to WSB, July 8, 1828 (Appendix F herein); "Biographical Register Being a Part of the Church Record Book Kept by Order of the Trustees," in "Church Record Book C" (MCHS), p. 61; Francis Voris to CWB, June 19, 1828 (LLIU); and CWB to Francis Voris, "undated Negotiation" (LLIU).

63. See (herein) WSB to CWB, June 19, 1828; and "Last Will and Testament" (Appendix H herein). WSB was given ten dollars by the trustees for a trip to Ohio on Sept. 17 and ten days later an additional five dollars while still in Ohio ("Account Book B," p. 156 [FC]).

64. WSB, "Last Will and Testament," in "Church Record Book A" (MCHS), p. 253 (Appendix H herein), and p. 26.

65. Ministry, Pleasant Hill, to Ministry, New Lebanon, May 18, 1829 (WRHS); "Biographical Register," in "Church Record Book C" (MCHS), p. 60. WSB's birthplace is given as Adams County, Ohio, in the "Pleasant Hill Shakers Roll Book, 1805-1887" (SPH), p. 22.

66. "Church Record Book A" (MCHS), pp. 26, 283-84.

67. "A Record of Visions, Messages and Communications Given by Divine Inspiration in the Society at Pleasant Hill, Kentucky, Vol. I" (WRHS), pp. 1-2. Concerning this period of Shaker history, see Clark and Ham, *Pleasant Hill*, pp. 43-47; and Andrews, *People Called Shakers*, pp. 152-76. For an analysis of the ecstatic activity, see Christy Ramage, "Shaker Spiritualism with Specific Attention Given to Spiritual Communications Received by the Society at Pleasant Hill, Kentucky, from 1838 to 1843" (M.A. thesis, Indiana Univ., 1978). Diane Sasson, *The Shaker Spiritual Narrative* (Knoxville, Tenn., 1983), contains an insightful discussion of the vision as a convention in the development of Shaker literature; see especially pp. 44-66.

68. "Record of Visions, Messages and Communications, I" pp. 1-2.

69. "A Record of Visions, Messages and Communications Given by Divine Inspiration in the Society at Pleasant Hill, Kentucky, Vol. II" (WRHS), pp. 94-97 (Appendix I herein). See "Pleasant Hill Shakers Roll Book," pp. 20, 65.

70. "Record of Visions, Messages and Communications, II," pp. 94, 97.

71. Ibid., pp. 95-97. Martin Runyon died two months after receipt of this message. The language and tone of this letter are typical of the spirit letters in the larger collection. Though contrasting in form, the letters are strikingly similar in content to the spirit drawings of this period received at other communities. See Edward Deming Andrews, *Visions of the Heavenly Sphere: A Study in Shaker Religious Art* (Charlottesville, Va., 1969); and Daniel W. Patterson, *Gift Drawing and Gift Song: A Study of Two Forms of Shaker Inspiration* (Sabbathday Lake, Me., 1983).

72. Often scholars using deprivation theory to explain the success of marginal religious groups focus only on the ways in which participants in such communities use ecstatic religion to advantage. The point must also be made that successful adjustments in one area may be accompanied by new problems in other areas. WSB and CWB would both be excellent subjects for psychohistorical investigations.

73. WSB was buried in the cemetery at Pleasant Hill. See "The deceased who sleep in the Shaker Cemetary" (MCHS). It is tempting to conclude that the weathered, tablet-shaped, broken headstone bearing the chiseled initials "W B" belongs to WSB, but there is no proof of the link. Willis Ballance was also buried at Shakertown.

74. Apart from Geiger's thesis on CWB and this author's earlier work, no previous scholarly use has been made of WSB's letters.

THE LETTERS

1. William Morton, a merchant in Lexington and long-term friend of CWB. See William Morton to CWB, Jan. 11, 1811, and Jan. 5, 1813 (LLIU). In the former letter Morton told of purchasing shares of stock for CWB in the Kentucky Insurance Company. On one occasion CWB took note of financial advice given by Mor-

ton: "Banks of Pennsylvania, and Banks of North America supposed by Mr. Morton to be best Banks to vest money in stocks in" ("Diary" no. 2, p. 33 [RCHS]).

2. Abner LeGrand, the son-in-law of William Morton, was also engaged in the commissions business in Lexington.

3. WSB's sister, who later married their cousin, Tucker Woodson, in 1832.

4. The farm of William and Priscilla McMurtry.

5. Dean was the black butler in charge of the household slaves at Chaumiere. See Harrison, "Chaumiere," p. 571.

6. Probably Hugh Kidder Meade, the brother of WSB's mother, who suffered a military injury in the War of 1812. See Peet, *Chaumiere Papers*, p. 78.

7. Possibly a slave or a horse.

8. The Shaker gristmill constructed in 1816 on Shawnee Run.

9. Dunlavy was one of the most prominent Believers at Pleasant Hill. Formerly a New Light Presbyterian minister, he remained in a position of religious leadership among the Shakers after coming to Shakertown. Author of the *Manifesto*, he also served as chief physician for the community and as first elder of the "gathering order." He died at West Union, Indiana, on Sept. 16, 1826. An observer's account of his death is found in John McLean, "Shakers of Eagle and Straight Creeks," *Shakers in Ohio*, p. 323. Of Dunlavy it was written: "We considered him a very faithful, and Good Man, and an able Minister of the Gospel, perhaps the ablest defender of *Mothers pure Gospel* of any man that has yet believed in the Western country." See Ministry, Pleasant Hill, to Ministry, New Lebanon, Apr. 27, 1827 (WRHS).

10. The blue pill was designed to produce a purgative effect. It contained triturated metallic mercury, honey of rose, glycerin, powdered althaea, and licorice. CWB wrote, "When the root of rhubarb fails of its intended effect, *the Blue pill taken*, half a grain at a time three or four times in the twenty four hours, appears to be necessary, and better than any thing else" ("Abridgment of My Advice," p. 16).

11. Patrick Henry Randolph, WSB's brother-in-law, the husband of Molly Byrd. The marriage was apparently very unhappy. One year after WSB's death, Molly's situation had not improved. Because of Randolph's philandering with women, including a slave girl, Molly and her daughters were reduced to desperate cir-

cumstances. Her poverty and distress were the subject of a letter from Powel Byrd to Evelyn Byrd, June 14, 1830 (FC). Powel especially regretted the fact that "the grand daughter of the great and illustrious Col Byrd has even been reduced to these streights."

12. Texas, Ky., a town twenty miles southwest of Pleasant Hill.

13. Ann Woodson, sister of WSB's mother.

14. A mutual acquaintance of Samuel Turner and CWB.

15. John Shain, a Believer who signed the covenant at the first organization of the church, developed a special friendship with the Byrds.

16. CWB apparently had some initial problems with the role of dance in worship which he subsequently resolved. He recorded the following verse favorable to such activity.

> Leap and skip ye little band,
> Shake your feet and fill the land,
> Oh! the comfort, life, and zeal,
> Little Shaker children feel,
> Shaking is the work of God,
> And it has to spread abroad.

("Diary" no. 1, pp. 22, 24 [RCHS]). For more on the role of dance and song in Shaker worship, see Edward Deming Andrews, *The Gift to Be Simple: Songs, Dances and Rituals of the American Shakers* (New York, 1940); Patterson, *Shaker Spiritual*; and Hilary Anne Selby, "Millennial Praises: An Historical and Theological Assessment of Shaker Hymns" (M.A. thesis, Indiana Univ., 1980).

17. Cousin of WSB, son of Samuel and Ann Woodson.

18. Nicholasville, twelve miles or more northeast of Pleasant Hill, was one of two locations (the other was Harrodsburg) through which the Shakers received and sent mail.

19. Here WSB originally wrote, ". . . when it was particularly inconvenient to you wounds my feelings whenever I think of it."

20. A Believer who for a time was part of the West Union community. During the period of WSB's residence at Pleasant Hill, Miller traveled back and forth to Busro. See McLean, *Shakers of Ohio*, pp. 322-25. CWB records the following comment: "Brother Henry Miller told me that for many years he has been divested of all doubt of *this* being the work of God, and of his continuance in it" ("Diary" no. 1, p. 22 [RCHS]).

21. Miller and Voris were visiting West Union at Busro, Indiana.

22. The vocational indecision of WSB's brother Powel was a source of great anguish to CWB. Powel was unhappy with the study of law and chose to make his living in the world of business.

23. WSB appears to have in mind the loss of humidity in a room heated by a wood stove.

24. William B. Page was the administrator of the Dismal Swamp shares owned by WSB. The correspondence involving those shares includes William B. Page to WSB, June 19, 1826; and to CWB, Dec. 17, 1826, and Dec. 5, 1827 (all in LLIU).

25. Samuel H. Woodson, brother-in-law of WSB's mother.

26. WSB's reference is to the early problems experienced by West Union in 1812, when the community was forced to abandon its village because of conflict between the military and nearby Indians. Some Shaker leaders counseled total abandonment of the settlement, but the community went against that advice. The decision in late 1826 to close the village was made by the leaders of the entire United Society of Believers. That decision was delivered by Richard McNemar. "Elder Elezar gathered all the people and after speaking a few sentences, he proceeded to read a letter that he had received from Elder Archabald, which contained the result of all his Labours and journey to the East, together with the conclusion of the Ministry at all the Societyes in the west, concerning all matters and things at Busro—The substance of which (In short order) was this—That it was universally thought and felt best, for all the people to rise once more and move away from Busro, and so abandon the place forever!" (McLean, *Shakers of Ohio*, p. 324).

27. Former wife of James Gass.

28. Author of *The Family Physician; Comprising Rules for the Prevention and Cure of Diseases; Calculated Particularly for the Inhabitants of the Western Country* (Cincinnati, 1826).

29. The publication in question seems to be the following item published in *The Supporter, and Scioto Gazette*: "The Frankfort [Ky.] Commentator states that Charles W. Byrd, Judge of the United States' District Court in this state, has joined the society of Shakers, residing in Mercer County in that state" (N.S. 6, no. 40, Nov. 16, 1826, p. 3).

30. Appointed Elder Brother at East Family, Oct. 2, 1826.

31. An unidentified acquaintance of CWB.

32. Thomas Smith Williamson, the son of William Williamson,

set up medical practice in Ripley, Ohio, after completion of his training. See Evans and Stivers, *History of Adams County*, pp. 640-42. CWB sought his medical advice in a letter of Jan. 1825 (LLIU).

33. Chaumiere, the estate of David Meade, WSB's maternal grandfather.

34. The Shakers of West Union who had abandoned the Busro village.

35. Azubah Harris, second eldress in East Family.

36. Elder Sister Charity Burnett, appointed First Eldress at East Family, Apr. 10, 1819.

37. Davis Dunlavy was appointed deacon at the East Family on Jan. 8, 1825. "March 30th, 1827 Davis Dunlavy met with a fatal disaster by a fall from a horse which broke his back, and eventually terminated his existence. (Though he lay perfectly helpless till the 23rd of Aug. 1832, at which time he expired.)" See "Church Record Book A" (MCHS), p. 70.

38. McNemar, who had been involved with the closing of West Union during the winter of 1827, was on his way back to Union Village.

39. Samuel Otway Byrd, WSB's half brother.

40. Jane Byrd, WSB's half sister.

41. A relative of Patrick Henry Randolph, WSB's brother-in-law.

42. Leonard Jones.

43. Maria Horsmanden Page, sister of CWB.

44. Susan Massie, sister of WSB's mother.

45. Matthew Houston, a New Light Presbyterian minister before becoming a Believer in 1806, was a prominent member of the Shaker community at Union Village.

46. This letter was written in an uncharacteristically scrawled or hurried hand.

47. Eleazar Wright was the name given to Richard McNemar by Mother Lucy Wright. See Andrews, *People Called Shakers*, p. 313.

48. Summer was the season for epidemic fevers in the nineteenth century. Febrile diseases were common in the Ohio River Valley from mid-July until the first frost. Yellow fever, malarial fever, ague—these and others produced incapacitation and death.

49. Nathan Sharp was a trustee at Union Village. He was in-

volved in the formal negotiations concerning the closing of West Union as well as the settlement of the problems at Pleasant Hill. See McLean, *Shakers of Ohio*, p. 325.

50. On May 27, 1827, Shields was released from responsibilities as Elder Brother of the First Order.

51. A mutual friend of WSB and CWB.

52. Kidder Meade Byrd to WSB, Sept. 24, 1824.

53. George Runyon, a deacon in the church and assistant trustee for several years.

54. Among the papers of CWB is a manuscript dated "Columbus. July 25. 1827" (LLIU) which describes an interview CWB conducted with a former Shaker from the community at Watervliet. The person had spent twelve years among the Believers whom he regarded as "a pure and holy people." When asked by CWB why he left the community, he replied, "I left them, because I was convinced I might enjoy as much religion in the world with more of liberty: theirs is a monarchical government, and there is but one consideration that holds them together, and this is, their having no children: it is not, as you suppose, the tie of religion. Altho they check and do not gratify their desire for the sexual intercourse, yet it is still the prevalent passion in both sexes: with a large majority this is evident, not only from the effects of dreams, alluding to that involuntary issue, which according to Deut. 22. 10. subjected the dreamer to a temporary separation from every thing sacred; but it is evident also from the candid confessions of almost all of them. To visitors, strangers, and to such as yourself, the best foot is always put forth, the best side is shewn." In addition to sexual preoccupation and deception, this former Shaker also accused the leadership of living in a grand manner by contrast with the "course, humble" life of the members. CWB regarded this testimony as proof of the Shaker capacity to restrain "carnal desire," but concluded, "In any light in which I can see the character of this informant, I view him, with the exception of what he says on the subject of the Believers abstaining from a gratification of the sexual intercourse, as being by far the most plausible and dangerous witness I ever knew to testify against our Society."

55. WSB to Doctor Williamson, Oct. 28, 1827 (Appendix D herein).

56. WSB was sensitive here to the damage that could be done to his father by unfavorable publicity.

57. Ephraim McBride, a Believer who subsequently joined the party of the apostates and brought suit against the village for compensation for his labor (Ministry, Pleasant Hill, to Ministry, New Lebanon, Nov. 28, 1828 [WRHS]).

58. Edmond Bryant, appointed Elder Brother of the First Order, Nov. 8, 1827.

59. Elder Sister of the First Order, appointed Nov. 8, 1827.

60. Caroline Bryant, Elder Sister of the First Order, who died Oct. 6, 1827.

61. A town in north central Indiana.

62. For the answers, written by Elder Eleazar Wright (Richard McNemar) of Union Village, to Williamson's questions, see Appendix D herein.

63. Elder Spinning from the ministry at Union Village, Ohio.

64. The site of Robert Owen's communitarian settlement in Indiana.

65. See Appendix E herein.

66. E.g., William Henry Harrison, John McLean, and John W. Campbell.

67. Elder Sister Betey McCarver.

68. Maurice Thomas, elder of the church for several years and physician at Pleasant Hill. His father Elisha was one of the first Shaker converts in the area.

69. Francis Voris to CWB, June 19, 1828; and CWB to WSB, July 8, 1828 (Appendix F herein).

70. On the outside of the letter CWB has written the following note: "from William he expresses his surprise at my intention as to the moiety of the McMutri tract in reference to our Society, and in turn has excited much surprise on my part and some unpleasant apprehension (dated the 14. of July 1828) in reference to the Society, not to him It however contains a direct message from brother Francis, the principal Deacon and manager for the Society in reference to the 6000 dollars of mine under his care and management, of a very satisfactory character."

THE APPENDIXES

1. "Questions to Believers" (LLIU). At the head of the first page of the first sheet is "Q 1st." See below, note 12. The title is written at right angles to the text on the margin of the fourth page of this sheet.

2. CWB traveled from Sinking Spring to Union Village, Ohio, a distance of approximately seventy-five miles.

3. The theological principle of "full redemption" was an idea gaining prominence among a variety of American religious groups in the nineteenth century. Premised upon a denial of the assumptions of total depravity, this position implied the possibility of full salvation, including complete sanctification or holiness. In particular, the Methodist followers of John Wesley looked upon this quest for perfection as the culmination of the experience of regeneration.

4. Luke 17:27.

5. I Corinthians 7:36.

6. Romans 7:15-17.

7. II Timothy 4:7.

8. II Timothy 4:8.

9. I Corinthians 15:51-52.

10. Benjamin S. Youngs, *Testimony of Christ's Second Appearing*.

11. Union Village, Ohio.

12. At the head of the first page of the second four-page sheet is written: "A 1st."

13. Romans 7:16-17.

14. I Corinthians 15:51.

15. I Samuel 13:14.

16. Ephesians 4:26.

17. The text of the manuscript ends abruptly without any punctuation. It appears that the remainder is missing.

18. "A Business Proposition" (LLIU). This proposal was delivered to CWB during his visit to the village. "Charles W. Byrd Present" appears on the MS.

19. The farm of William and Priscilla McMurtry, subsequently purchased by the Byrds.

20. A neighbor and property owner near the village.

21. For whatever reasons, CWB did not accept this proposal.

Two months before his death in 1828, however, he attempted to arrange a trade of his home in Sinking Spring for Taylor's tract (CWB to Francis Voris, "undated Negotiation" [LLIU]).

22. Mercer County Court House Deed Book, no. 14, p. 80, Harrodsburg, Ky.

23. Alexander Robertson, holder of an original patent in Samuel Woods's settlement with John McMurtry, father of William.

24. David Epperson, a landowner adjacent to Pleasant Hill, who sold sixty-nine acres to the village in 1836.

25. A creek probably named after Littleton Coghill, a neighbor of the Shakers, who appears in the village records as a witness to a land transaction on June 2, 1814 ("Church Record Book B" [MCHS], p. 247).

26. On the margins of the deed are the following notations: "McMurtry deed To Byrd's"; "Fee & Tax pd."; and "Exd & Dcld to F. Voris."

27. Copy of original in WSB's hand (LLIU), sent as enclosure with WSB to CWB, Oct. 30, 1827.

28. John 5:39-40.

29. See John 5:38-47.

30. Acts 8:30-31.

31. Malachi 2:7.

32. I Corinthians 6:19.

33. John 20:29.

34. John 21:25.

35. John 14:12.

36. Thomas Cleland, *Unitarianism Unmasked; its Anti-Christian Features Displayed: its Infidel Tendency Exhibited; and its Foundation Shewn to be Untenable; in a Reply to Mr. Barton W. Stone's Letters to the Rev. Dr. Blythe* (Lexington, Ky., 1825), p. 170. Cleland's attack upon Shakerism is located in chapter 8, entitled "Tendency of Unitarianism to Deism—Associated with Mahometanism and Shakerism," pp. 144-70.

37. John 10:35.

38. Philippians 2:6.

39. I Corinthians 15:28.

40. Copy of original in CWB's hand (LLIU) addressed to "William S Byrd, Pleasant Hill, Near Harrodsburg, Kentucky."

41. Lavinia was the servant who had been involved in the care of WSB during his childhood.

42. CWB seems to have been citing from memory the opening section of Book 4 in William Cowper's *The Task, A Poem in Six Books* (London, 1785). That section, entitled "The Winter Evening," reads as follows.

> Hark! 'tis the twanging horn! O'er yonder bridge
> That with its wearisome but needful length
> Bestrides the wintry flood, in which the moon
> Sees her unwrinkled face reflected bright,
> He comes, the herald of a noisy world,
> With spattered boots, strapped waist, and frozen locks,
> News from all nations lumbering at his back.
> True to his charge, the close-packed load behind,
> Yet careless what he brings, his one concern
> Is to conduct it to the destined inn,
> And, having dropped the expected bag, pass on.

Cited from John Bruce, ed., *The Poetical Works of William Cowper*, 3 vols. (London, 1909), 2: 97-98.

43. Elder David Spinning from Union Village.

44. Youngs, *Testimony*, pp. 457-58. In this section of his volume, Youngs argued that the pattern of history is progressive. "That which established the testimony of Christ in his first appearing, is neither necessary nor proper to be repeated in confirmation of the work of his second appearing: but the testimony itself is a sufficient confirmation of the work; as much as the tree is a confirmation of the fruit which it beareth."

45. Watervliet, or Niskeyuna, located northwest of Albany, New York, was the site where Ann Lee and her early followers settled after arriving in America.

46. New Harmony and Busro were located in western Indiana in an area CWB regarded as dangerous to the health of the residents.

47. *Niles Weekly Register*, edited by H. Niles and Son and published in Baltimore.

48. See *Scioto Gazette*, N.S. 1, no. 51 (Feb. 14, 1828): 1. The *Gazette* was published at Chillicothe, Ohio. The law case referred to was "John Heath vs Nathaniel Draper, State of New Hampshire, Sup. Court, Grafton County, Oct. Term 1810," which dealt with the issue of property claims by persons leaving the society. The editorial apology on page 3 relates to the delay in publishing the text of the case.

49. The text of the law case is printed in the *Daily National Intelligencer*, Dec. 1, 1827, according to the *Investigator*, p. 38 (see "Introduction," note 51, above). It also appears in the *Investigator*, pp. 48-51.

50. See *Scioto Gazette*, N.S., 1, no. 52 (Feb. 21, 1828): 1. More than two columns are devoted to a description of Judge Desassur's decision in a case involving an objection to a witness on the grounds that his religious beliefs were not "orthodox."

51. *Niles Weekly Register*, 3rd ser., 10, no. 18 (June 28, 1828): 282.

52. Probably a copy of the original written in CWB's hand (LLIU). It displays no signs of sealing wax. In addition to the same address as the letter in Appendix E, this contains the following return address: "Charles W. Byrd, Sinking Spring, 1828."

53. Francis Voris to CWB, Oct. 27, 1827 (LLIU).

54. Francis Voris to CWB, June 19, 1828 (LLIU).

55. On May 31, 1828, Henry Baldwin of Pittsburgh gave a public speech in which he spoke in favor of the tariff of 1828. Baldwin was the chairman of the Committee on Manufactures in Congress. The text of the speech is given in full in *Niles Weekly Register*, 3rd ser., 10, no. 18 (June 28, 1828): 290-94.

56. A discharge of fluids, possibly dysentery.

57. CWB also recorded other advice from Burgess concerning the care of teeth. He wrote, "Mr. Burges says that a hand brush will sometimes actually restore the enamel to a tooth when a part is broken off—he speaks from medical knowledge, and from personal experience" ("Advice to My Children," p. 18).

58. Danville, Ky., ten miles southeast of Harrodsburg.

59. Benjamin S. Youngs to the Ministry, New Lebanon, Sept. 8, 1828 (WRHS).

60. Endowed with a practical, shrewd sense.

61. See above, "Introduction," note 51.

62. Ibid.

63. A Believer at West Union who joined the opposition party at Pleasant Hill. He left the society in 1829. See McLean, *Shakers of Ohio*, p. 340.

64. A Believer at Pleasant Hill who visited West Union in the spring of 1826. Barnett left the Shaker community on Aug. 15, 1828.

65. Richardson Whitbey joined his brother John in the chal-

lenge to the leadership at Pleasant Hill and with him was forced to leave the community. He subsequently married Camilla Wright and took part in the communitarian effort at Nashoba, Tennessee. See J.F.C. Harrison, *Robert Owen and the Owenites in Britain and America: The Quest for the New Moral World* (London, 1969), pp. 167-68.

66. WSB, "Last Will and Testament," in "Church Record Book A," p. 253 (MCHS).

67. Wilhite served as a trustee for Pleasant Hill from 1810 to 1844.

68. Concerning the will of CWB, see Burtner, "Charles Willing Byrd," pp. 239-40.

69. John Page was the husband of Maria Horsmanden Byrd, the sister of CWB. Page served as the administrator of a trust of $500 given by Mary Willing Byrd.

70. The evidence concerning CWB's attitude toward slavery is mixed. See Helen M. Thurston, "The 1802 Constitutional Convention and Status of the Negro," *Ohio History* 81 (1972): 15-37. CWB's inheritance from his father included "his man Tom & little Jack White & his choice of two negro girls" ("Will of William Byrd III," p. 58). From his mother he was willed "his man Ned" ("Will of Mary Willing Byrd," p. 350). Slavery was not allowed in the Northwest Territory, but it appears that CWB may have held slaves in the hands of his relatives in Kentucky. He was not a radical abolitionist. When evaluating the advantages of West Union, Ohio, over Sinking Spring, he listed "No free Negroes" among the advantages of the former location ("Diary" no. 3, p. 35 [RCHS]). It is impossible to determine if Lavinia, mentioned above, was black. WSB's decision to free any slaves under his control was an additional source of conflict with family and relatives.

71. A citizen of Mercer County.

72. Bradshaw, a resident of Mercer County, with his wife and other parties, sold 149 acres to the Shakers on March 27, 1832 ("Church Record Book B," pp. 262-63 [MCHS]).

73. "A Record of Visions, Messages and Communications Given by Divine Inspiration in the Society at Pleasant Hill, Kentucky, Vol. II" (WRHS), pp. 94-97.

74. Father William Lee, brother of Ann Lee.

Index

155